MW00939779

As He is
So we are
In this world

1 John 4:17

Copyright © 2017 AJ Sherrill
All rights reserved.
ISBN: 1979776210
ISBN-13: 978-1979776219

Thanks Y'all.

There are so many kind humans to thank for shaping my journey this past season. I'll keep it to a few short lines. Erinn and Nick Jacques, thanks y'all. You inspire me to sacrificially follow Jesus. Mars Hill Bible Church, thanks y'all. I'm grateful for our common life and your faithful desire to seek the Kingdom together. Rob Bell and Shauna Niequist (and others I'm unaware of who helped conceive the directions), thanks y'all. Staff of Mars Hill Bible Church, thanks y'all. It's a joy to work and play together. James Love and Jonathan Merritt, thanks y'all for quality feedback and editorial work. Elaina and Eloise, thanks y'all. My life was analog before you. I love you. Father, Son, and Holy Spirit, thanks y'all (*tres personae, una substantia*). Your love created, redeemed, and is renewing the world. I believe this to be true with everything in me.

Kind words.

Many years ago, I was part of a team that scrawled these seven words on a dry-erase board in the offices of Mars Hill Bible Church in West Michigan. When AJ told me he was going to bring the directions words to life in a book, I was delighted. These words are infinitely more meaningful with the depth and vision that AJ brings to them. This book is a helpful vision for Christian life, far beyond the seven words that started the journey.

Shauna Niequist, NYT best-selling author of Present Over Perfect and Bread & Wine

When it comes to a path of discipleship, we tend to either opt for an allegedly organic, unstructured approach or go all-in on a rigid one-size-fits-all program. What A.J. invites us into is a rich, integrated way of following Jesus that pulls us in all the right directions. And to top it off, he refuses to let us treat it as a solo project. Biblical, multi-disciplinary, and deeply pastoral, this is an incisive and insightful guide into the flourishing life of Christ.

Glenn Packiam, Associate Senior Pastor, New Life Church
Author, Discover the Mystery of Faith

The Christian gospel assumes, and honest hearts confirm, that the human condition is one of disorientation—we know instinctively that we are not (yet) what we are made and meant to be. If you are looking for a resource to help you re-orient into the person you were meant to be, let the the formation practices AJ articulates in this volume be your guide. You, your tribe, and God's world will be the better for it.

Scott Sauls, senior pastor of Christ Presbyterian Church in Nashville, Tennessee and author of From Weakness to Strength

We are bombarded with so much noise and so many messages, many of us are searching for clear direction. AJ Sherrill has created an incredibly accessible but still profound guide for life with God in this confusing age. With humor, wisdom, and pastoral skill, Sherrill avoids the temptation of many Christian leaders to over-simplify the call to Christlikeness to mere formulas or principles. Instead, he carefully guides us into the practices that will draw us into greater communion with the living Christ and one another.

Skye Jethani, author of What's Wrong With Religion?
and co-host of The Phil Vischer Podcast

Discipleship is less about arriving at the correct destination and more about orienting your life in the right directions. This is the liberating message of AJ Sherrill's new book—a 360-degree review of the Christian life that is chock-full of pastoral wisdom and incredibly readable. Sherrill's ideas can help you overcome the obstacles that stymie spiritual growth. I can attest to their transformative power because I've experienced them firsthand.

Jonathan Merritt, contributing writer for The Atlantic and
author of Learning to Speak God from Scratch

Contents

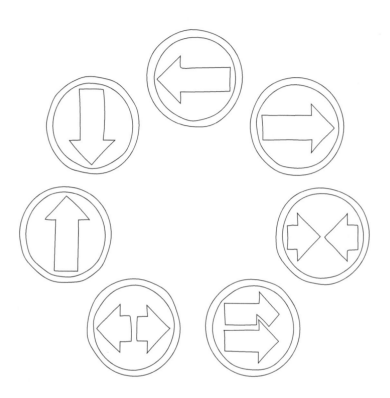

Elephants in the Sanctuary

Faith is the opening of all sides and at every level of one's life to the divine inflow.
Martin Luther King Jr.

Elephants fill the sanctuary. And very few Christians (especially us, pastors) want to name them. The Church is rife with ills, inconsistencies, and hypocrisies. This has always been true—just read one of Paul's letters in the New Testament. Each letter is a cocktail of encouragement for ways they are nailing it and also correction for ways they are, um, not nailing it. The aim of this work is to name one of the larger elephants present in the Church, and then attempt to solve it for the sake of human flourishing.

The Church has a formation problem. Plain and simple.

EXPANSIVE IDEA

I meet people every week who have attended a church for decades, and attest to little spiritual progress. After years of church commitments, programs and projects, many Christians don't feel *different*; they just feel *older*.

Week after week the implicit message is come to church, sing some songs, hear a sermon (and a long one at that), and then get back to life as usual. Sophisticated churches might offer a guide to personal bible reading, perhaps some liturgical prayers, and ongoing small groups. But let's not kid ourselves. The deep work of transformation cannot be solved by programs alone.

Having pastored from the west coast of Southern California to the east coast in New York City, from the deep south of Atlanta charm to the winter north of Grand Rapids, I can testify that the formation problem is significant. This book cannot alone solve the problem. But it does aim to point in seven directions toward some necessary solutions. We begin by turning our attention toward three endearing personas.

Penny, Popeye, and Pepe Le Pew

In 1994, Anfernee Hardaway emerged as an elite (and very tall) point guard in the National Basketball Association. His nickname was "Penny." Alongside Shaquille O'Neal, he was nothing short of spectacular, particularly if you lived in Orlando, Florida—which I did. Around the time of his athletic emergence arose an action figure depicting him. It was known as the bobblehead. A bobblehead figurine has an oversized head comparative to the toy's body. Basketball fans arriving to a then-packed Orlando arena were greeted at the entrance with a complementary Penny bobblehead. Fans loved it. But it's also useful as a metaphor. It seems many Christians today function as theological bobbleheads. We have amassed more knowledge than we will ever apply. Sermons, books, blogs, podcasts, tweets, profiles, 24-hour news cycles—all of these contribute to the information age we are steeped in. And that's not all bad; it's just incomplete.

Many people have come to believe an illusion that we have a brain that is separated from the body—as if they are distinct realities. In truth we have an incredible system of neurons (around 100,000,000 in fact) constantly flowing from our brains into our bodies. Therefore, our brains are not distinct from our bodies. Our brains are constantly being distributed throughout our bodies! To be a human in search of God is not merely being a head on a stick. We are created to love God with all of our beings.

Popeye, the childhood cartoon, ate spinach. Lots and lots of spinach. Oddly enough, spinach is a robust source of protein. Per calorie, spinach contains more protein than ground beef—score for the vegetarians! So when Popeye ate the green leaf, his muscles expanded to meet whatever the physical challenge demanded in the moment. A preoccupation with strength left one wondering about whether Popeye ever felt the urge to develop his mind and his heart. This is the state of many Christians who advocate ardently for social justice. I regularly meet followers of Jesus who are so thoroughly developed in their will (or strength, or action) that the mind and heart go unattended. We can forget to follow after God in life. To be a human after God is to be much more than a will accomplishing projects for God. We were created to love God with all of our beings.

3

Pepe Le Pew was born in 1945. A cartoon skunk from France, he was incessantly in search of love and appreciation. His emotions gushed. He was all heart, all of the time. As they say, "He wore his heart on his sleeve." Pepe serves as an adequate metaphor for many Christians today who sing love ballads to Jesus, but have yet to develop their minds and wills to search after God. Richard Foster, in his seminal work, *The Celebration of Discipline* opens with the challenge that what the world needs most today is deep people.[1] To be a human after God is to be much more than a heart gushing love ballads. We were created to love God with all of our beings.

Penny, Popeye, and Pepe Le Pew expose our propensity to partially seek God. The Shema (Deuteronomy 6:4-9) is the central corrective for a lopsided faith. In it, worshipers are called to love God holistically—head, heart, and hand. Instead, we often gravitate toward our strengths and neglect our weaknesses. This creates an unhealthy pursuit of God over the course of a lifetime. I've met people who love to sing to God, yet would never consider mentoring a refugee. I've seen social justice advocates who serve the poor, yet view prayer as optional. I've studied under theologians who can exegete Paul, but disbelieve in the spiritual gifts that Paul himself claims are active in the local church. Following Jesus is a holistic pursuit. We were meant for an expansive spirituality that grows into fullness as we engage our entire beings in pursuit of God's Kingdom.

Expansive

This little book is an attempt to make one claim: the human experience is dynamic. You are not a static entity. If you ever feel stuck, this book is good news. If you ever feel shame, this book is good news. If you ever feel lost, this book is good news. If you ever feel forgotten, this book is good news. If you ever feel lonely, this book is good news. If you ever feel marginalized, burdened, addicted, bored, trapped, cynical, depressed, weary . . . this book is very good news.

In the beginning God made you and me—we—very good.

It is clear, from the macro structures of the world to the micro caverns of the human heart, that our inherent goodness can seem distant, fractured, and hopeless. The Scriptures call this "the fall." Christians from the East (known as Orthodox with a capital "O") remind us to fear not, for we have not lost God's image...but we are in search of God's likeness. This search, then, is the meaning of life. It's the quest behind all of our earthly endeavors, not just Sundays from 9:30-11am. School, work, marriage, singleness, feasting, community, solitude, rest . . . all have something to do with our pursuit of Christlikeness. The claims of this work are attempts to help followers of Jesus redeem God's original longing for their lives—namely, to be like God.

The human experience is dynamic, not static. This means no matter how stuck we may feel we are all capable of change, breakthrough, development, evolution . . . call it what you like. But make no mistake, God is after the transformation of your whole life, and your transformation is a microcosm that tells the macro story of what God is doing in all of the world. God invites us to stretch and expand ourselves. The traditional word for this invitation is *discipleship*.

Homo Viator

Christianity is a movement. Seven directions help us jump into the transformative stream of this movement. The core truth of Jesus' followers is that we are a people in process. In Christ, we know what we've been liberated from. And we know of an already/not-yet Kingdom we are being liberated to. But from here to there is the journey of transformation. The Latin phrase *homo viator* invites us to accept that we each have a pilgrimage to make. We are all (existentially speaking) on the move. This book affirms that the Christian life is graced. Therefore, it is not about earning, but it does require effort. In other words, transformation requires cooperation with God. This book is about being honest about that transformative journey. This book is about being willing to take the next step. This book is about growing into God's fullness—Christlikeness.

If you are anything like me, you know how easy it is to practice that which we excel at, and call that discipleship. Dallas Willard named this propensity, "The Great Omission." For example, some feel equipped at prayer, while others feel most at home when serving the poor. Some feel alive when reading books, while others seek to feast around the table in community. This book is about suspending either/or mentalities when it comes to following Jesus. Each chapter offers a unique direction to assess how expansive our discipleship really is. Most of us settle for a partial orientation toward God's Kingdom when what is needed is comprehensive discipleship. When we give ourselves to a holistic spirituality, it expands our humanity. We were created to stretch.

Just as God invited humans to take the earth forward and stretch it culturally, we must remember that we, too, are a part of that culture, and are designed to be stretched into Christ-likeness day after day after day. This expansive "anthropology" is the meaning of human flourishing. You were not created for spiritual management. Essentially, to grow we must pay greater attention to each of the following directions: **Inward, Upward, Withward, Outward, Backward, Forward, and Downward.**

Structure

Each chapter of this book has a consistent structure: Story, Scripture, and Scaffolding. I begin each chapter with a story. Narrative has a way of penetrating our hearts. Jesus knew this and told stories all of the time. The story serves as a knife to break open the manna of each direction. Each chapter is also tethered to sacred Scripture. The claims made in this book spring from years of toiling in the text. The more we read the text, the more the text can read us. Over the years I have found Scripture to be a trustworthy source of inspired texts to guide my journey toward transformation. I have fallen in love with Scripture because it chronicles the spiritual ancestry that I have been grafted into by the mysterious power of the Holy Spirit. Scaffolding is the third component of each chapter. Just as the scaffolding on a building helps draw out the character of any given structure, in this section of each chapter, I draw out what each direction specifically means. This will help the reader break down the material and put it back together. Last, each chapter concludes with an invitation to lean further into the direction.

A friend of mine once told me that every culture is the result of either *intention* or *allowance*. Culture is either created intentionally or permitted (allowed) unintentionally. Think of it like a garden. Hydrangeas are beautiful. They are the result of intentional sowing. Weeds are unintentional. If they are allowed, they will take over the culture of the garden. Much of life amounts to existential drift—allowance. We allow ourselves to snooze the alarm far past our intention when we set it. We allow ourselves to fill the cracks of the day with social media. We allow ourselves to get sucked into binge watching televisions shows we won't remember. We allow ourselves to settle for mediocrity and spiritual management, hoping that attending a Sunday gathering for one hour per week will magically impart all the dynamism we need.

The flourishing life is a matter of radical intention. We must join God in co-creating the culture of our lives. And the culture of life begins with the human heart. What kind of culture are you creating in your life this season? What specific aspirations, dreams, and intentions are you clear about that will guide you toward the kind of holistic life you long for? Are you living with awareness of following Jesus in each direction? Which direction from above is most natural for you? Which direction demands the greatest effort from you? As you read each chapter, pay attention to the direction(s) that are easy to omit.

Your formation matters to the world. Those who change the world for the good take their formation seriously. The seven directions in this work will help us step further into our personal formation. As you are formed further into Christ's likeness, you embody hope that a new world is possible. But let's not kid ourselves—formation is hard. The 20th century essayist, G.K. Chesterton, rightly pointed out, "Christianity has not been tried and found wanting; it has been found difficult and not tried."[2]

You already bear God's image. May you passionately live in search of God's likeness. Jesus showed us the way and made it possible through the power of the cross and resurrection. Open yourself in every direction and participate in God's expansive work in your life. May your personal journey bear witness to the redemption narrative God is writing in all of the world.

TWO

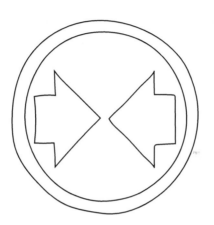

Inward

The desert journey is one inch long and many miles deep.
Inward is the only direction of travel.
Amma Syncletica

Magic. It happens. And often when least expected. It happened for Justin Vernon in the late winter of 2006. The year was neither particularly remarkable, nor an utter letdown. Facebook went public, Pluto was dwarfed, Crash won best picture, and, perhaps most tragic of all, James Blunt's dirge, "You're Beautiful," was forever etched into our pre-frontal cortexes. While, years later, Taylor Swift longed to get "out of the woods," that cold Wisconsin winter, Justin Vernon longed to get in.

Battling mononucleosis, a string of poker losses, and breakups with both his band (DeYarmond Edison) and his girlfriend, Justin packed it up and headed north for some isolation therapy.[3] He picked up odd jobs for his father, chopped wood, drank booze, and binged films. Several weeks into this pseudo-monastic rhythm he entered a mental clearing. The voices dwindled, the sound settled, and solitude went to work. The creativity flowed and the songs started spilling out. The result was *Bon Iver*. Thanks be to God!

Magic. It happens. And often when least expected.

Wonders are formed in the dark, when no one is watching. As it turns out, solitude is not a foe, but a friend. Mark Twain penned his classics in a farm shed in rural New York.[4] Isolated from his family in the main house, they would blow a horn to summon his presence for dinner. J.K. Rowling vanished from social media while writing the Harry Potter novels. Twice a year Bill Gates chooses solitary confinement for the purpose of clarity. He calls these times "Think Weeks." Due to his penchant for solitude, the renowned physicist Peter Higgs could not be immediately located after being announced as the Nobel recipient in 2013. We admire the output of authors like Twain and Rowling, leaders like Gates, and scientists like Higgs, yet remain largely unaware of their time spent in the wilderness of solitude, stillness, and silence—three ingredients that made each of their contributions possible. There are connections between depth and solitude, clarity and stillness, identity and silence. Sadly, within our increasingly meritocratic-technocratic world, many of those connections are being severed. And we are subconsciously compliant every step of the way. We reap what we sow.

Rejecting depth, we seek immediacy.
Fearing shame, we flee solitude.
Snubbing silence, we prefer noise.
Neglecting stillness, we've become human-sized fidget spinners.

It is no wonder we often feel disconnected from our true selves. Journalist David Brooks sums this up well:

We live in a culture that teaches us to promote and advertise ourselves and to master the skills required for success, but that gives little encouragement to humility, sympathy, and honest self-confrontation, which are necessary for building character . . . you spend a lot of time cultivating professional skills, but you don't have a clear idea of the sources of meaning in life, so you don't know where you should devote your skills, which career path will be highest and best. Years pass and the deepest parts of yourself go unexplored and unstructured. You are busy, but you have a vague anxiety that your life has not achieved its ultimate meaning and significance.[5]

Plato's ancient aphorism has never felt more relevant than it does today: *know thyself*. Yet even that invitation demands interpretation. Who precisely am I to know? And who are we? What does it mean to be human? Is identity achieved or received? Attractive as it may be, the cure is not discovered in the next self-help seminar or social justice cause. The cure is simpler, more profound, and closer to home than that. It begins by reaching inward. It is that place inside each of us that Jesus taught to return to over and over. He referred to it as an inner room (Matthew 6:6), a place to retreat and withdraw to time and again in order to recover our true selves. Personal intimacy with God is the well that nourishes us to best contribute to society. Which brings us to something very important—your name.

_____ **SCRIPTURE** _____

In those days Jesus came from Nazareth of Galilee and was baptized by John in the Jordan. And just as he was coming up out of the water, he saw the heavens torn apart and the Spirit descending like a dove on him. And a voice came from heaven, 'You are my Son, the Beloved; with you I am well pleased.' (Mark 1:9-11 ESV)

A perplexing Scripture if ever there was one. The baptism of Jesus raises all sorts of difficult questions such as: Why was he baptized? Did he (not) have the Spirit before this moment? Did the Gospel writers actually observe this? What does it actually mean that the heavens were torn apart? Was it *like* a dove, or a real dove? Was the voice that spoke audible to others? Theologians are all over the map on these questions. As adventurous (or mundane) as pursuing these questions may be, for the sake of the inward direction let's focus on verse 11 —

"You are my Son, the Beloved; with you I am well pleased."

Beloved is translated from the Greek word, *agapetos*. In short, the Father is self-disclosing a brand of love that is reckless, sacrificial, and undignified. The closest relationship humans have to comprehend the profundity of this love is that between a parent and child. Have you ever wondered why Jesus, who is the eternal second person of the Trinity, is referred to as "Son?" I think this brand of love has something to do with it. Notice that the Father's love is not dependent on the Son's performance. It simply is. Up until this point in Jesus' life, he has lived rather unremarkably. Well, except for that virgin birth bit. That was kind of a big deal. After that his life had been rather obscure, hidden, and ordinary.

Probably picking up the family trade as wood and/or stone worker, Jesus attends Synagogue like a good Jew, observes the festivals, and quietly goes about his life.

Then this happens. In a nanosecond the prophecies of the past move toward fulfillment. The Kingdom of the future begins to arrive in the present. After what must have felt like aeons of radio silence from God (known as the Inter-Testamental period—a debatable theory), all of a sudden the metaphorical lights are turned on, the volume is maxed out, and it becomes clear to all who surround the Jordan that God has not "left the building."

Baptism was the first act in Jesus' public ministry. In this first act he did not perform a miraculous healing, but he received; he did not engage the world with renewal activity, but took on the form of human passivity. Baptism was the foundational act that would fuel the ministry of Jesus. If you want to heal others, you must be healed through waters of life. If you want to give generously, you must first receive. Jesus models the way forward for the people of God.

EXPANSIVE IDEA

Jesus' first initiative in public ministry was not to make a name for himself. His first initiative was to receive a name for himself. And that name is *Beloved*. For those who seek to missionally "be love," they are wise to first "be-loved."

And this is where we pivot to the Church. In the New Testament, the Church is referred to by the same name, *Beloved*, no less than 66 times. Jesus is the beloved one through which the people of God access belovedness. If the Father is for the Son, and the Son is for the world, then all of creation is lathered with inherent belovedness. If only we would receive it. Some have rightly referred to this as active passivity. It is the notion that we must actively choose to posture ourselves in passive surrender. God does not coerce us into love. God woos us by knocking gently on the doorframe of the soul. Our role is to actively answer that knock, and passively permit God entrance into our entire lives. This, then, is the beginning point of expansive spirituality: giving God a radical welcome into the chambers of our being, and allowing the Holy Spirit to fill us completely—body, mind, and spirit.

Hear the words of God over your life:

Therefore be imitators of God, as beloved (agapetos) children (Ephesians 5:1).

Since we have these promises, beloved (agapetos), let us cleanse ourselves from every defilement of body and of spirit (2 Corinthians 7:1).

As God's chosen ones, holy and beloved (agapetos), clothe yourselves with compassion, kindness, humility, meekness, and patience (Colossians 3:12).

The 19th century Danish Philosopher, Søren Kierkegaard, purportedly made the startling claim, "The only real distinction between men is that one knows he is loved while the other does not."[6] Could it be that simple? Could the spiritual life really begin by recognizing the scandalous love of God dispensed in all of the world, including our own heart? Can it be that everything good from us flows from first realizing our belovedness in Christ?

There is a final Scripture that haunts me. In the first chapter of the book of James, he writes,

"Do not be deceived, my beloved (agapetos)."

It is striking that deception enters the equation when it comes to our belovedness. As strange as it seems in the 21st century, post-enlightened worldview, Scripture invites us to consider the presence of societal forces that conspire against us receiving and believing our true names. These forces (i.e. spiritual warfare) continuously reverberate within that you lack; that you're insufficient; that you're not enough; that if only you would just prove yourself before God and others, then you could be taken seriously. Henri Nouwen discerned these forces at work in his own life and fiercely combatted them, writing, "You have to listen to the voice who calls you the beloved, because otherwise you will run around begging for affirmation, for praise, for success. And then you're not free."[7] Could it be that our foundational calling to become like Jesus begins by understanding that we must not go out and *get* love, or *earn* love, or *achieve* love. Rather, we must freely receive love, that is, to be-loved! That is your name. From that place everything flows. The truest path to lasting mission in the world is through genuine communion with God.

This is best received through three actively-passive pursuits to which we now turn our attention: solitude, stillness, and silence.

_____ **SCAFFOLDING** _____

The inward direction is not a novel trajectory. Jesus models the inward direction time and again in his earthly ministry. As early as Matthew 4, before launching his public ministry, Jesus engages the forces of evil. Essentially, his battle in the wilderness is a transformative renewal of the mind (Romans 12). In each temptation Scripture re-centers him in reality—belovedness. Noticing he has everything he needs in his belovedness, the seductions of Satan in the form of appetite, approval, and ambition pale in comparison to what he already has in the Father. Forty days of solitude prepare him to engage the world—even his enemies—with love. It is the same with us. We need solitude to remember our true names, and to live into our true story. We are beloved.

One of the greatest obstacles to solitude is the persistence of internal shame. Subconsciously we avoid solitude due to fear of resurfacing the past. We live in an externally-shaming culture perhaps like never before. This is evident through politics, through social media, through face-less emails, and so forth. Over time it is easy to develop a kind of "script" that echoes in our heads. These scripts are false narratives that we repeat over ourselves. For example, I'll never be _____. I'll always fail in _____. No one will ever love me because _____. The inadvertent comment made by a colleague at work, or a neighbor down the street, or a family member around the table hits a raw spot in your past, and then you find yourself rehashing the same internal monologue you've tried so hard to forget. It, therefore, makes sense why we dodge solitude. I mean, who really wants to deal with those false scripts all of the time? It's better just to remain busy, you think to yourself. Do you notice how this can easily get you off of God's script? Namely, that you are beloved.

Alluding to our fear of solitude, Friedrich Nietzsche once wrote, "When we are alone and quiet, we fear that something will be whispered in our ear. So we hate silence and drug ourselves with the social life."[8] Our perception of God matters tremendously. Many in society live largely unaware that the God who sent the Spirit to equip Jesus for a life of love is the same God that pronounces belovedness for all who will receive it. In solitude, we need not fear a God who responds to our brokenness by covering us in grace rather than exposing us through shame (Genesis 3:21). The whisper, then, is not a repudiation of our personhood, but an elevation of our status, and expansion of our humanity into further Christlikeness. This is what it means to look inward and find God waiting within. Not just waiting, but pronouncing your name.

In Matthew 6 Jesus invites us to go into our "inner room" (Greek: *tameion*) and pray there in secret. Geographically, in the 1st century he may have been referring to a pantry-like room in the center of a dwelling. It is there that food items could stay cool from the Middle Eastern heat. This room ensured privacy and sincerity in prayer, as there were no windows to flaunt one's piety. However, it is not a stretch to imagine Jesus was also referring to the inner dimension of one's life. To go into the depths of who we are—dreams, longings, fears—and pray from that place. Solitude provides a spacious place for us to recenter on who we are and to pray in light of our beloved identities. This should be routine in the followers of Jesus. Twentieth century psychologist, Erik Erickson, once explored how we must learn to lead ourselves. He believed leadership meant gathering yourself together into a single point rather than letting yourself be dispersed everywhere into "a cloud of electronic and social input."[9] Unlike Justin Vernon, you don't have to move to a cabin in the Wisconsin woods to get these benefits, but even a short amount of solitude on a daily basis lets us hear our thoughts.[10] Further, it opens us to God's. Augustine purportedly once said, "I have read in Plato and Cicero sayings that are wise and very beautiful; but I have never read in either of them: Come unto me all ye that labor and are heavy laden." Jesus' promise here is to take our shame (*heavy laden*) and give us a name (*rest*).

The year was 1944. Christmas in Berlin was particularly dark that year. Maria Von Wedemeyer was engaged to the Lutheran theologian, Dietrich Bonhoeffer, whom the Germans imprisoned for conspiratorial activities. His letter to Maria was the final one she would receive before his execution. In it, he wrote about the ostensible presence of God and people within solitude:

> These will be quiet days in our homes. But I have had the experience over and over again that the quieter it is around me, the clearer do I feel the connection to you. It is as though in solitude the soul develops senses which we hardly know in everyday life. . . . Therefore you must not think that I am unhappy. What is happiness and unhappiness? It depends so little on the circumstances; it depends really only on that which happens inside a person.[11]

In solitude we discover we are not alone. We are inhabited by the Presence of God. And this Presence reminds us of our names. We, in the name of Jesus, are the beloved.

If solitude invites us into a kind of space, stillness invites us into a kind of time. In that time, we allow the waves of the mind to rest. The Greek mystic, Saint Diadochus, likens the mind to the sea:

> When the sea is calm, fishermen can scan its depths and therefore hardly any creature moving in the water escapes their notice. But when the sea is disturbed by the winds it hides beneath its turbid and agitated waves what it was happy to reveal when it was smiling and calm; and then the fishermen's skill and cunning prove vain. The same thing happens with the contemplative power of the intellect.[12]

The problem isn't that the waters of life are murky. The problem is that they are raging. Only when those waves have calmed can we clearly see through the waters into our inner depths. Until then, our lives remain tumultuous and, thus, we remain self-unaware of what is happening beneath the surface. Solitude is the gift of space, and stillness is the gift of time. With the gift of time, we can detach from the freneticism called "my everyday life" and gain clarity about ourselves.

People often talk about "checking in" with various technologies. The consequence of "checking in" is that we are simultaneously "checking out" of whatever is happening around us. Checking in also means checking out. More and more, emerging generations are checking out of the 3-dimensional life directly in front of them, and checking in to a 2-dimensional existence mediated by flat screens. That is not to say that the social media world is inherently evil, because it most assuredly is not. It is to say that our commitment to flat screens, technology, and the myth of multi-tasking is leading us away from stillness and honest self-reflection. It is no wonder we feel disconnection from our deepest desires and settle for immediate substitutes that over promise and under deliver. It is no wonder we feel over-connected and under-communed. It is no wonder that we may just scratch our heads in 30 years and think, "What did it all mean?"

Several exhaustive years into hosting the Comedy Central television program, *The Daily Show,* Jon Stewart confessed, "I have two speeds in my life—pedaling a hundred miles per hour uphill to try to stay up, or sitting at home on my couch with a glazed doughnut on my lap staring at a Knicks game. I need downtime to refill the reservoir. I don't have much of a life outside (of work). It is all consuming."[13] Ten years ago this speed of life may have been the exception for the indefatigable few. Sadly, it is the confession of what seems to be a growing majority. Again, it is no wonder the waters of life feel murky. We have not created rhythms that help us to say no to that which depletes life in order to say yes to creating a kind of life where clarity, rest, and conviction become the norm.

Nouwen calls this kind of intention toward life discipline. His understanding of discipline was anything but suffocating. Discipline, for Nouwen, was a gateway to resource human flourishing. His working definition of the term meant to "prevent life from filling up."[14] Discipline is simply the act of creating space within time for God to act. Commitment to a rhythm of stillness opens our minds and hearts to more. Preventing handheld devices from absorbing every inch of our down time is a much-needed discipline in the technocratic age. We must *proactively* create this kind of life; otherwise we will live much of our life *reactively* to the tyranny of the urgent. Emails, requests, social media, calendar engagements, etc. must be prevented from choking out all of our free moments.

MIT professor, Sherry Turkle, provides prescient insight to our cultural moment, which I think applies not only to our relationships with one another, but our prayer life with God: "Our mobile devices seem to grant three wishes, as though gifts from a benevolent genie: first, that we will always be heard; second, that we can put our attention wherever we want it to be; and third, that we will never have to be alone.[15]

She continues in her work, *Reclaiming Conversations,*

These days, average American adults check their phones
every six and a half minutes. We start early: There are now
baby bouncers (and potty seats) that are manufactured with a
slot to hold a digital device. A quarter of American teenagers
are connected to a device within five minutes of waking up.
Most teenagers send one hundred texts a day. Eighty percent
sleep with their phones. Forty-four percent do not 'unplug,'
ever, not even in religious services or when playing a sport or
exercising. All of this means that during the dinner hour, the
typical American family is managing six or seven simultaneous
streams of information. Scattered about are laptops, tablets,
phones, a desktop, and of course, in the background, a television, perhaps two. College students who are using any form of
media are likely to be using four at a time.[16]

Whereas technology has advanced our common life in many
profound ways, it is critical to assess the extent to which we connected to the world, yet disconnected from the self. Stillness is an
invitation to reclaim access to our inward direction. As Malcolm
Muggeridge, a journalist who converted to Christianity late in life,
once said, "It is possible to make a little clearing in the jungle
of our human will for a rendezvous with God."[17] When creating
space and time (i.e. discipline) to seek God, we discover a God
who never relents from seeking us. In this place of less clutter, we
find ourselves most. Brennan Manning called it the discipline of
"showing up."[18] Solitude and stillness are the beginning to self-dis-
covery—to recognizing, realizing, and reclaiming our names as
the beloved children of God. Yet there is one more ingredient we
must add before concluding this chapter—silence.

I've pastored long enough to know the largest elephant in any
church that goes unmentioned—prayer. None of us feel very good
at it. That is why our commitment to Scripture is so helpful in
cultivating a robust prayer life. The Psalms provide us prayers to

utter when we don't have the words to express our joy, our pain, our longing, our failure, and our doubt. I've grown in prayer by first praying other people's prayers who were much further along on the journey. But there is a missing component in all of this. Even if we feel able to articulate our feelings, ideas, and longings to God, we struggle to be with God. Silence, then, is a spiritual depth that few Christians ever mature in to. Silence is a gift. Silence is a means of reclaiming our belovedness. For example, many people wrongly assume silence must mean absence, or lack of intimacy. But what if silence meant the opposite? What if silence with God means that, in Christ, the Trinity has no accusation to utter against you? You are loved. You are accepted. You are more forgiven and desired than you could possibly imagine, and more heard than you dared dream. What if silence, like an elderly couple staring into each other's eyes over dinner, with nothing left to say, implies intimacy and connection and not distance? What if silence is what comes after all of the words, when words fail to properly convey the depths of the human heart? This is the gift of silence. And this is the same gift we prefer to ignore because of our addiction to noise. Now that's tragic.

In a popularized TED talk on listening, Julian Treasure describes some of the cultural realities that got us to this moment:

1. The world is noisy and we've become immune to it.

2. To dodge ambient sounds, we've retreated into isolated headphone sound bubbles.

3. Sound bite culture galvanized by social media has reduced our capacity for patience.

4. Conversation is replaced with status updates.

5. In a noisy world filled with 24-hour news cycles, shock and awe grab our short attention spans best.

6. It is now harder to pay attention to subtlety because we are used to cacophony.[19]

If there was ever a need to reframe the gift of silence, it is now. Silence is the quieting of the waves of life so that we may see to the depths of who we are, and then live from that place of honest self-reflection and truest longing.

If we are going to live the way of Jesus well in the 21st century, it must begin with inward attention—cultivating life with the Holy Spirit within. Permitting God to begin making us whole is the first step to expansive Christianity. The inward direction confronts our illusions and reminds us of what is true: we are the beloved in Christ. From this place of healing we can begin reaching out to life around us, inviting all of creation to participate in a renewal we can testify of in ourselves. This is an invitational life. This is a life that stretches into new directions. In the words of Nouwen, "We retreat from the noise for solitude, stillness and silence in order to return to the world whole, with love to give away."[20]

Truly, to be love, we must first be loved. And, according to God, that is our name. This is the beginning of expansive spirituality, also known as Christianity.

EXPANSIVE PRACTICE ────────────────────

The Jesus Prayer

Set aside a few minutes each day, and pray the most utilized prayer in Church history:

"Lord Jesus Christ, Son of God, have mercy on me."

Connect the prayer with your breath. Breathe in God's life, and breathe out one phrase at a time. As the 7th century monk, John Climacus taught, "Let the name of Jesus cling to your breath, and you will know the meaning of stillness."[21]

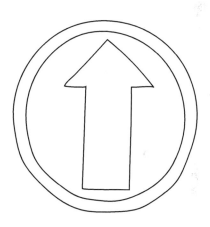

THREE

Upward

> We should love God as a smitten lover of the beloved.
> A lover who is passionately in love would say:
> 'But that is everything. That is my life.
> There is nothing but that; the rest does not count,
> it is non-existent.'
> *John Climacus*

One of the highest moments of my life occurred while lowest to the ground. The air felt so holy that I can remember wanting to peel back the carpet and crawl below. But let me back up.

It was the winter of 2009. I was on a sabbatical[22] not knowing whether vocational ministry would be my future. Leading up to that moment was a long, dark, cold season of spiritual wasteland. A desert. A wilderness. Some call it deconstruction. Others call it the dark night of the soul. All I knew was that the absence of God was more palpable than the presence.[23]

Nearing the end of the sabbatical, after reading many books chased by bottomless cups of coffee, my over-caffeinated brain was stuffed and my under-emotional heart was dry. Too much information, too little transformation. Too many ideas, too few experiences.

A new friend recently told me he thinks God would be happier if we had half as much knowledge and twice as much obedience. That's probably true. In any case, I needed something real from God. Something beyond my theories. And I needed it desperately.

During this season, in the evenings, Elaina attended a church that had recently been planted in the heart of Atlanta, Georgia. She would return home with joy, passion, and a renewed sense of life to begin the week. Meanwhile I remained at home, too depressed to get off of the couch, and too cynical to follow my bride to a worship gathering. So, she brought the worship gathering to me. Well, sort of. She handed me a CD. Remember those? For weeks it sat staring at me from my desk, tautly wrapped in its transparent packaging.

Sunday night came around again (as it always does) and we found ourselves in an argument as to why I wouldn't go with her to church. It was odd to her that a former pastor on sabbatical would refuse to set foot in a worship space on a Sunday evening. In retrospect it wasn't odd; it was a vicious cocktail of insecurity and pride—two vices that keep us far from breakthrough. Funny the things that we often need most, we seek least.

So off—alone—she went. And there—alone—I sat.

Twenty minutes after her departure I summoned the strength to get off the couch. Dragging my spiritual apathy to the car, I went for a drive through the Georgia hills. Glancing down, in the passenger seat, a familiar CD magically appeared, still tautly wrapped in transparent packaging. I had an idea who put it there. So I did the unthinkable: I unwrapped the CD and slid it into the slot. Like millions of Christians before me, I surrendered to the voice of Chris Tomlin. It was a moment of cerebral weakness. But that weakness led to revival.[24] Three minutes into the album found me in tears. The opening song was called *Awakening*. How appropriate.

Arriving home I ejected the CD from my car and reinserted it in my living room. It was there, alone, that one of the highest moments of my life occurred while lowest to the ground. The air felt so holy I can remember wanting to peel back the carpet and crawl below. On my face I found God again. Or maybe God found me. Or maybe it was both at the same time. Who knows? His absence dissolved into a consuming presence. For the first time I felt something real, something true, something unbelievable: that I was beloved. In an effort to sort out my role in the world, I felt the Spirit whisper into me that my greatest role to play wasn't a career, but a posture. And that posture is face down before the feet of Jesus. Eureka!

EXPANSIVE IDEA

This is the upward direction. It stretches us beyond our tendencies to look down, and expands our capacity to encounter a transcendent God on earth.

SCRIPTURE

You, God, are my God, earnestly I seek you;

I thirst for you, my whole being longs for you,

in a dry and parched land where there is no water. (Psalm 63:1 NIV)

I begin most days like many people—in the shower. I have friends who tell me they awake to the alarm and immediately roll onto their knees in prayer. That's not me. I wish it was, but it's not. I'm far too weary to be so holy at that time of day. So a few years ago I started raising my hands in worship as the first act of the day—in the shower. I view it as an act of holy defiance against my preposterous inclination to believe I am the Lord. No matter the season of life, I've determined the best way to flourish is to begin in adoration. No matter what I am facing, the fact that I have breath means there is at least *one* thing I can be grateful for. Gratitude is the antidote to apathy and despair. I believe that not in theory, but in lived experience. Adoration is the first act of my day. Worship is the origin of joy. This subtle act sets the tone and trajectory for all that follows. Upward matters.

In my brief years on this earth, I've come to the conclusion that adoration opens us to greater receptivity in life. It is very difficult to be in agreement with what God wants for us when the postures of our minds, hearts, and bodies are closed in on themselves.[25] Sometimes our hearts and minds guide the postures of our bodies. And sometimes our bodies transform the postures of our hearts and minds. This is why people often raise their hands in worship gatherings. This is why people often open their hands in the benediction. This is why we sometimes kneel down during music or when reading the Scripture. This is why we eat the elements of the Eucharist table every week. We use our bodies to inform our hearts and minds to open, to become straightened, and to receive God. To be invited to raise the hand while worshiping isn't manipulation, it's invitation. When we open our entire selves to God, the Spirit can flow freely in and through us. And the Spirit moves most along paths of least resistance.

The Psalms are fanatical about the upward direction. They compose a book of worship. In them, the word praise is utilized in seven various forms.[26] What is particularly instructive here is how involved the body is in worship. This is true both personally and communally. Worship is embodied devotion. It is multifaceted. In Paul's letter to the Romans (12:1), he is clear that worship is holistic as we aim to orient our entire selves in devotion to the Kingdom of God. I am struck in the Psalms by how involved our bodies are to this end. We are not gnostic, disembodied souls seeking to escape our flesh in order to truly worship. We are humans—mind, heart, soul, and body. As integrated beings we utilize one aspect of our humanity to pull the others toward God as well. Below is a chart to demonstrate just how embodied worship is in the Psalms.

PRAISE (v.)	MEANING	ACTION	PSALM
Hallal	Praise God, Sing Hallelujah!	Shout and celebrate	113:1-3, 150:1
Yadah	Extend a hand	Lift hand into air	63:1, 107:15
Towdah	Lift hand in avowal	Lift hand into air	50:14, 50:23
Shabach	Shout in a loud tone	Cry out and clap	47:1, 145:4
Barak	To bow down	Kneel	95:6, 34:1
Zamar	To pluck an instrument	Play music	21:13, 57:8-9
Tehillah	To sing or laud	Using voice and instruments	22:3

Thus far, I am simply presenting a case for worship as an embodied (and not just emotional or cerebral) reality. This is nothing novel. It is derived from Scripture, when God commands us to love Him with all of our heart, soul, and strength (Deuteronomy 6:5). This is neither coercive nor oppressive. Worship is for our good, and bears fruit in the world. God is after our entire person, because flourishing is a holistic endeavor. It means that every moment in life matters: church, work, family, school, and yes, even the shower.

SCAFFOLDING

The upward direction begs the question, *"What is worship for?"* True worship *informs* our minds theologically, *transforms* our hearts in desire for God's Kingdom, and *reforms* our wills to live out a better story—God's story. Worship, then, with the community of believers, the Church, is not optional, but essential to our formation into Christlikeness. It is holistic, shaping our minds, hearts, and wills. Consider the gift that holistic worship is to humans alone.

> On the one hand, corporeal (physical) but unintelligent creatures, like the sun in its orbit or matter serving as substructure for life, offer a sort of cosmic liturgy to God by their obedience to the natural law; on the other hand, incorporeal but intelligent creatures, like angels, offer their liturgy to God by surrounding the throne in constant praise; however, with the appearance of human beings a new kind of liturgy is possible, a response that is both corporeal and intelligent. It is a liturgical response made with both body and spirit.[27]

For this reason, the 4th century theologian Gregory of Nazianzus, refers to the human experience as hybrid.[28]

Let us not forget that worship was a central passion of the early Church. During the horrific reign of Diocletian, Christians were jailed and martyred for faithfulness in worship of the Triune God. They were charged with acting against the orders of the emperor, and their reply was: "We have been celebrating what is the Lord's . . . and what is the Lord's cannot cease."[29] Worship has always been a response to the revelatory God. It cannot be stopped. God is that good. Worship is an enfleshed manifestation to onlookers that God's presence swirls among the community and that the praise and glory due God cannot and will not be denied. In essence, worship is the natural human response to God's incredible self-disclosure.

Soaking > Sprinkling

No, this is not a position on baptism (even though it could be). It's a position on liturgy. James K.A. Smith's seminal work, *Desiring the Kingdom*, presented liturgy as an unavoidable facet of life.[30] Everything is liturgical: everything between going to the mall or gathering as the church. Everything is constantly forming and reforming us into a kind of image. Therefore, all facets of life are considered liturgy. Let's consider this as it relates to the Sunday gathering at the local church.

The question is not, "Are we or are we not liturgical on Sundays?" The question is, "Does the Sunday liturgy sprinkle or soak us in the story of God?" Much of the contemporary church has been a (well-intended) quest to sprinkle the story of God in ways subtle and diluted. In an effort to grow congregations and avoid offense, liturgy is often scaled back to mirror one's everyday life rather than pulling the community into a profound story, that the Church refers to as the Gospel, which they most likely will not explicitly receive anywhere else throughout the week. *Our gatherings should be other-worldly*. Other-worldly not as a means of escapism, but disruption from the typical routine, and immersion toward a new reality that best equips us for faithful living beyond Sunday. It was Jesus who said, "My Kingdom is not of this world" (John 18:36). He did not mean that it cannot be previewed anywhere in the world, but that the origin of what God is doing in the world begins in a realm beyond the world—a realm the Scripture refers to as Heaven. Heaven is other-worldly. We must, therefore, regularly seek that realm in order to better remember both who we fundamentally are, and to guide our desires to faithfully pursue that hidden realm on earth in all that we do.

Everywhere we look, society is recruiting our loyalties toward various stories. The Sunday liturgy, then, is meant to so deeply form us, that we are not seduced into false scripts of "the good life." These various false scripts always over promise and under deliver. I think this explains why so many of us live in a constant state of anxiety, disappointment, and exhaustion. Perhaps the antidote, or at least part of the antidote is formational worship on a regular basis, an upward experience that disrupts our temporal proclivities.

Scholar Jean-Jacques von Allmen believed, "Christian worship is the strongest denial that can be hurled in the face of the world's claim to provide (humans) with an effective and sufficient justification of their life. There is no more emphatic protest against the pride and despair of the world than that implied in Christian worship."[31] When the church sings and proclaims, "*Jesus is Lord*," it simultaneously renounces, "*Caesar (and ourselves) is not.*" As we make this pronouncement, then, we renounce illusions. We soak ourselves in this reality every Sunday as a community, that we may set aside living in lies personally on Monday. This is upward.

Again, the question is not, "Are we or are we not liturgical on Sundays?" The question is, "Does the Sunday liturgy merely sprinkle or deeply soak us in the story of God?" Those who are most deeply immersed are best equipped to remain faithful to the story of God throughout their lifetime. The Church that flourishes in the 21st century ceases to be consumed with the question,

"How do we best attract them?" and instead asks, "How do we best form them?" The answer to the question should be contextual but always Gospel-centric.

The Trellis and The Vine

In 2009, liturgy came back into fashion. At least it did in the circles I run in. My guess is that usage of the term "liturgy" among Evangelicals has sky-rocketed from virtual non-existence to cliché since then. Conferences, books, albums, etc. . . . so many endeavors in the Western Church today point to a "new liturgy." It is somewhat obsessive. One of the primary questions floating around in 2009 was "Are you liturgical or charismatic?" I had a good answer to this. It was (and is) "Yes."

I think the flourishing church in the days ahead will devote themselves to a worship expression that is ecumenical,[32] resourcing the best of Christian traditions. What is essential in this devotion is not motivated by attraction, but formation. I am not referring to musical genre and style. I am referring to structure.

Every garden needs a good trellis. A trellis is a framework of dead wood. There is no inherent life in it. Its goal is to support life and also to prevent life from growing in any and every direction. It provides structure for life, but also boundaries for when life grows out of hand and is no longer in cohesion with the whole. This is liturgy. It is never an end, but always a means. Structure supports the mission, never the other way around.

Whether it is "high" liturgy, or "low" liturgy doesn't matter for the purpose of this chapter. What matters is a framework for gathering the local church in a way that soaks the people of God deeply into the central story of God's redemptive plan. We need a trellis for this, otherwise we get distracted and obsessive about being innovative and novel as a means of attraction and provocation.

But we also need life—a vine. This living vine among us is the Holy Spirit. We need environments where the Holy Spirit is free to roam, to heal, to speak, to nudge, to empower, to inspire, to transform. Does the local church to which you are committed reflect and value that?

In sum, a trellis without a vine is just a stapled block of dead wood. A vine without a trellis becomes chaotic and fosters a brand of individual expression that, over time, subverts the unity of the Body of Christ. Worship in that environment gets messy quickly. This is what Paul was getting at in Romans 12-14. An incredible outpouring of the Holy Spirit occurred among the early church, but well-intentioned people were perverting it for their own advancement.

For this reason I refer to myself as a liturgical charismatic. My aim is to co-create environments for both process (liturgy) and breakthrough (charismatic). The word *charismatic* is charged; I get that. It derives from *charis*, the Greek word for grace. What I am meaning is that I am open to God's extravagant grace in ways that are beneficial and biblical. I am open to life. I am open to the vine growing among us. Otherwise, it's just dead wood.

The Church herself must stretch in the days to come. We must go beyond our denominational comfort zones. God is not just experienced in the liturgical form, but also in spontaneous breakthrough. God is not only revealed in charismatic manifestations, but also in contemplative silence. God's character is not only revealed in emotive ballads, but in ancient hymns. The future of the flourishing church is ecumenical and soaks her people in the story of God. Local churches that are agile in integrating various expressions of the Triune God are best positioned for multi-cultural community and mission in the world.

EXPANSIVE PRACTICE _____

Prayer as Worship: The 4-fold path

Worship is holistic and multi-dimensional. It takes into account the whole person (body, mind, spirit) and the whole God (Father, Son, Spirit). Among many things, true worship adores, confesses, gives thanks, and intercedes. However, our worship (personal and communal) often majors on one or two of these facets, while neglecting the others. This four-fold worship paradigm, though not exhaustive, is helpful for both personal and corporate worship. Consider setting aside 2 minutes each day for the next month, and integrating these four questions as a path of daily worship:

1. Do you have a specific moment of the day where adoration of God takes place?

   The Psalms' seven words of praise above exhibit Scripture's dedication to adoration. Praise and adoration are central forms of worship. I have found that when I least feel like praising is when I most need to, and when it most psychologically heals me. Again, there are times where simply putting our bodies into certain positions influences the posture of our hearts. For me it is in the shower with hands held high in praise to begin my day. In the midst of the cold, February mornings in Grand Rapids, Michigan, I am rarely in top form to praise. The grey clouds alone are enough to make me want to sleep the alarm over, and over, and over until lunch. *Yadah* (extend the hand), then, becomes the first order of my day to suppress the urge to give into the mood of the weather. The joy of the Lord is my strength. I will choose to look up into the Heavenly realm and declare the wonders of God with an outstretched arm as a subtle defiance of the gloom (e.g. weather, circumstances, disappointments, sickness) that surrounds me. This is adoration to a God worthy of all glory, honor, and praise in every season.

2. Is *confession* a part of your daily rhythm?

Confession has a bad reputation these days, but it is a central form of worship. Confession is not self-shaming. It's self-owning. In sincere confession we own our brokenness and are met by a God who restores—again and again and again. The prayer, "*Lord, have mercy*," has become a frequent prayer throughout my day. My fragility, weakness, and propensity to drift is reason enough to confess my need for God's restorative presence.

Several years ago I began praying with the Anglican *Book of Common Prayer*. I find that praying the prayers of wiser people from ages past can teach me the art of intimacy with God. In it there is an old prayer that has found a home in my heart. A few of the lines read:

Most merciful God (reminds me of God's restorative gentleness)

I confess I have sinned against you in thought, word, and deed (comprehensive brokenness)

By what I have done (sins of commission)

And by what I have left undone (sins of omission)

This prayer does not heap burning coals on me. Instead, it serves as an honest invitation to see the human story as a mixed bag of joy and pain, despair and hope, loss and victory. It provides me with a release valve to do something with the frustration that I feel inside. In this prayer I have somewhere to put all of my disappointments and depression. Believing the mystical claim that somehow Jesus gathered the sin of the world into himself on the cross, this prayer actualizes by faith that reality. Martin Luther called it the "happy exchange."[33] Jesus takes my shame, sends it to the pit of hell, and restores me in joy. Confession gets a bad reputation. But it shouldn't. Properly understood, confession sets us free and leads us upward.

3. When is intentional *thanksgiving* integrated into your prayer life?

One of the greatest omissions of my journey is perhaps taking God for granted. How often do we stop to acknowledge that oxygen is a gift? That gravity is free? That we are right now flying 67,000 miles per hour through the universe? And that the sun averages being around 93,000,000 miles away from earth—incredibly the same distance necessary for life to survive. How often do we stop and grasp the profundity that God chose to enflesh and dwell among us to liberate us for everlasting flourishing? Thanksgiving is the facet of worship that best restores me to what I am prone to take for granted.

The word *Eucharist* means thanksgiving. In our communal gathering, the Eucharist enters us deeply into the story by receiving the story deeply into us. Eucharist is a thankful restory-ing. Thanksgiving propels our hearts upward. In this act of worship we are reminded that God is the giver of all good things. Thanks be to God!

4. Is intercession a value in your spirituality?

Scriptures tell us that we are priests (1 Peter 2:9, Revelation 1:6). What?! That word hits us differently depending on our backgrounds. Simply stated, our priesthood means we straddle the Kingdoms of Heaven and earth. Let's not downplay our oddity in the world. The Church (*ekklesia*: called out ones) are those peculiar people who stand between two moments, longing for the Kingdom of Heaven to further become the reality of earth. But let's be clear - the Church does not hate the earth. The opponent of the Church is not society, even when society opposes the Church. The Church wages against principalities and powers which manifest at various times and places in the world. We, the Church, must refuse to be enemies with people who see reality differently. The Church contends for all of creation. Our ministry to the world is not condemnation, but advocacy and intercession for her full renewal. Jesus taught us this pattern and is present with us to see it comes to fulfillment.

Walter Wink once said that history belongs to the intercessors.[34] Could this be true? Might we have more authoritative power than we realize? As priests God is working through us to bring about restoration. The question is whether or not we care about what God longs to do in the world, and whether we are open to being those people through whom He does it. Do you intercede for the world? Your city? Your neighborhood? This is one of the ways we worship, believing God acts on behalf of the cries of people. We believe God invites us to participate in renewal. We are not pawns. We are participants in the Kingdom of God.

Consider integrating this 4-fold path of worship into your daily life. Be creative with it. Make your prayer life your own as you seek intimacy with God. This is our upward direction. It subverts our tendency to only look down toward the ground. Worship raises our gaze to the hidden realm of God's Kingdom and restores our sight to then see what God wants to accomplish on earth.

FOUR

Withward

Friendship is rentable in Tokyo.
Chris Colin

Jiggs went missing. Imagine a 22-pound beagle lost in the Canadian woods. His owner, Suzanne Simard, couldn't find him anywhere. She's now a professor of Forestry at the University of British Columbia. At the end of her search she discovered the dog stuck at the bottom of an outhouse . . . covered in poo. That's right. A pool of poo. #PoP

Digging him out of the disgusting, um, refuse, she noticed an intricate roots system entangled underneath. The system was so wide and vast one could walk on it. It was roots upon roots upon roots. Underneath the dung the forest roots had configured in all conceivable shapes, colors, and sizes. At that moment, amidst the poo, Simard says she first discovered her reason for existence. An unlikely location for that moment to occur.

Since that time, her career yields this central claim: What is happening *down there* is as complex and beautiful, as alive and connected, as what is happening up here. In fact, maybe it's even more connected. And maybe the ways we are choosing to live on earth in the 21st century are a step back from the way in which we were created to flourish.

Check this out. Early in her foresting career she tracked trees that were uprooted and sold, ensuring new trees were planted in their place. During this season of her life, she tracked some interesting patterns. For example, if she removed a Birch tree, the nearby Douglas Fir would die soon after. Now, up until this point in the forestry world, it was believed that different species of trees competed for sunlight. It's called "shading out." The tallest tree wins. Darwinian forestry. It is, to some extent, true, particularly between different species. But there is more to it. Shading out implies that trees don't work together for mutual upbuilding. It implies a lack of connection, that they each use their own root system independent from other trees. Her research began to reveal that this theory is not the whole picture.

To prove her point, she conducted an experiment injecting a foreign gas into one tree. Some time later that same foreign gas was present 47 trees away. Forty-seven! Her research unearthed the possibility that trees (irrespective of species) share resources, are deeply connected, and act like a kind of underground family.

But it gets even more relational than that.

Let's talk fungi. All foresters know fungi can't photosynthesize. Trees can photosynthesize. This means fungi can't convert light energy from the sun into chemical energy for food. The quandary is that fungi need food. Fungi are heterotrophs, which means their energy is derived by breaking down organic molecules from other living things.[35] What fungi do have are minerals. They extract minerals up from the soil. And minerals are what make the bark of a tree reality. But here is the problem: Although trees can photosynthesize to make carbon, their roots are often not wide enough to get the minerals necessary to make bark. And so how does a tree get the minerals it needs to manifest into the bark of a tree? They make trade deals with the fungi. What?!

Trees need minerals. Fungi need sugar. So they share! Some refer to this forest dynamic as the "wood wide web." Contrary to popular opinion, trees are not autonomous competitors, nor are they tribal in the sense of caring exclusively for their own species. They are relational. They are cooperators.

Apparently, it kind of works like this: Fungal roots stretch up toward the tree with their tubes and say to the tree, "Hey, I'm in your zip code, wanna work together?" The tree then softens its roots to make room for the fungal tubes to wrap themselves into place. And they make the exchange—sugar for minerals, minerals for sugar. Everybody wins.

EXPANSIVE IDEA

> Here is the point: Underneath your feet, at the core of creation, the earth is teeming with interconnectivity, relationship, and cooperation. I wonder if the earth is trying to teach us something about how we are supposed to live "up here."

Maybe relational intimacy is woven into the fabric of the world. It makes me think that every time I walk into a church gathering I should be asking, "How do I move more closely toward these people?" It makes me curious about how humanly dignifying eye contact and kindness is with the cashier at the store. It makes me question the pervasive habit of filling my ears with buds that connect me to music but disconnect me from the sounds of humans in the world around me. We were created for interconnectivity. We are wired for relationship. The forest is an amazing teacher.

SCRIPTURE

At the beginning and at the end of Jesus' earthly ministry, he's doing the same thing: creating relationships. Spirituality is always personal, but never private. We are called to walk the journey of faith on this planet in community. Consider these texts:

Beginning of Jesus' earthly ministry:

Going on from there, he saw two other brothers, James son of Zebedee and his brother John. They were in a boat with their father Zebedee, preparing their nets. Jesus called them, and immediately they left the boat and their father and followed him. (Matthew 4:21-22)

End of Jesus' earthy ministry:

Near the cross of Jesus stood his mother, his mother's sister, Mary the wife of Clopas, and Mary Magdalene. When Jesus saw his mother there, and the disciple whom he loved standing nearby, he said to her, 'Woman, here is your son,' and to the disciple, 'Here is your mother.' From that time on, this disciple took her into his home. (John 19:25-27)

Jesus begins ministry, not by forging the Kingdom on his own, but by inviting seemingly random people to follow him into a new kind of family dynamic. In fact, some of the disciples literally left the trade of their blood relations to follow him into a different way of life. Fast-forward about 3 years. Jesus is hanging on a tree, dying a humiliating and excruciating death.[36] In his dying breath what is he doing? He is creating new family bonds. The Apostle Paul named this dynamic *new creation*. Something previously not there, through the blood of Jesus, mystically happens. What!? That is how essential relationships are to the God who created them.

At the beginning and end of Jesus' ministry, he is connecting people to himself and each other. Later this would be the *ekklesia* (church). The Church are those "called out ones" from the world who organize their lives around the Presence of God in community. They are the ones called to bear witness to what God is doing in all of the world: namely, drawing all nations unto himself. This occurs best through relational dynamics. God models this dynamic in Trinity, and invites the world to participate in the Trinitarian life. I could pause here and write volumes on the Trinity, but others have done that much better than me. Suffice it to say, when the Church speaks of Trinity, she means that God, in essence, is relationship. Therefore, the Church, drawn into this Triune God, is called to reflect the relational dynamic that is always happening in Trinity. Spirituality is always personal, but never private.

There has been much written on the application of the blood of Jesus. Some view it as a sacrificial offering, purifying from sin those who claim it over their lives. Others see the blood of Jesus as merely the tragic consequence of getting in the way of worldly empires. But consider this possibility: What if the blood of Jesus also reminds us that a new bloodline—a new family—was being formed by the Triune God? Maybe Jesus' blood means that he was serious in creating a new family dynamic amongst those who follow him. Surely this is (partly) what early Christians who often compromised their nuclear family fidelity had in mind when refusing to renounce Jesus as Messiah.[37] Replete throughout the New Testament is the Greek word, "*uios*" (pronounced way-os), meaning brothers and sisters. At the core, we do not relate to the Church as fellow strangers, acquaintances, or colleagues. Rather, the Church is family. Imperfect family, no less, but family still. The blood of Jesus defines our relationality. This means that what binds us together transcends our race, color, gender, and politics. It's far more fundamental than that. What binds us together is Jesus' blood. That is all we need in common to relate as family at the deepest level. What if the Church began to take that holy mystery seriously?

This strikes at the heart of two pervasive paradigms in the Church. The first is church "as event." In this paradigm, individuals generally gather to consume sermon content, sing some songs, and then evaluate after as to whether or not they "liked" it. The other paradigm is church as "network." The meaning of the church in this paradigm is to provide me with beneficial contacts that can advance my personal agenda (e.g. career). The network mentally views the church as a communal means to an individual end, rather than a kind of end in and of itself.

Ronald Sharp, professor of English at Vassar College, teaches a course on the literature of friendship. In the course he lectures, "Treating friends like investments or commodities is anathema to the whole idea of friendship. It's not about what someone can do for you, it's who and what the two of you become in each other's presence."[38] When the church's, as network, cultural framework is imported into the local church, the congregation is reduced to a mechanism for use and then discarded when expedient. This is not exactly what Jesus lived and died for. The paradigm Jesus establishes in the New Testament is "Church as family" for all of the reasons listed above. I wonder what might change in any given church if this viewpoint was tweaked.

How then, do we begin to access the meaning of the church at a deeper level? The following 3 commitments play a part in disrupting our tendencies to engage the church as a commodity, inviting us into deeper Christlikeness.

The first commitment a flourishing church must regain is rootedness. Someone once asked Saint Anthony the desert father, "What must we keep in order to be pleasing to God?" And Anthony answered, "Keep what I tell you. Whoever you may be, always keep God before your eyes. And whatever you do, do it from the witness of the Holy Scriptures. And in whatever place you live, do not leave quickly."[39] Did you catch that?

In whatever place you live, do not leave quickly.

Another translation reads, "Do not leave easily." Sociologists are mystified about the transience of emerging generations. Of all the good globalism has deposited, commitment to locality has suffered a net loss. In the introduction to one of my previous books, *Enneagram and the Way of Jesus*, I highlight the stark reality that it is normative for adults under the age of forty to move multiple times among multiple states (or countries). Whereas this kind of mobility is in some ways a cause for celebration, in the service of relational depth it is the cause of lamentation. Relationships, like good wine, take time. Imagine removing a tea bag from one cup of hot water to another every 30 seconds. Beverage dilution would result. I wonder if the same could be said about what is happening in both Church and society today.

Social media has reinvented the term "friends" to span the relational range from someone I know and love to someone I've vaguely heard of. In our time, we boast of having more "friends" than ever before while surrounded by empty chairs around the dinner table. It has been said that ours is a generation living in quiet desperation.

The lack of rootedness many of us experience has dire implications for the Church. When pastoring in Manhattan between the years of 2011-2016, the average attender remained in the city less than 3 years. I used to tell newcomers to the city to join a local church and become a member, even if you do not intend to stay long term. The reason for this is that we are members of the global Church through our covenant with a local church. Therefore, wherever you are and however long or short you plan to stay, always opt into being known by the people you are with. It is far too easy to opt out of meaningful relationship, vulnerability, and accountability when you suspect you won't be living in the same place in a few years time. This is one of the reasons we settle for paradigms such as church as event and/or network. Our expectations of others and ourselves are diluted as a consequence of transience. Despite the illusion of community that vehicles such as social media can project, millions struggle with profound loneliness.

EXPANSIVE IDEA

Recent studies show that loneliness is registered in the same part of the brain as physical pain. This means the human body takes loneliness quite seriously. And loneliness is a significant issue today from the farm to the city.

In a city like New York, with millions and millions of people, the statistics of relational displacement and disconnection are staggering. It is no wonder that people end up in various addictions as an attempt to feel something in life. In an age of individualism, perhaps the greatest compliment a local church can be given is not a visitor liking the music, or the preaching, or even the liturgy. Rather, it's the experience of warmth, welcome, and hospitality. Let us never forget that sound theology, which is necessary, is not what brought the Roman Empire to its knees. The Romans actually believed Christians to be atheists.[40] It was the radical hospitality of the early Church that won over the hearts of people. Robust theological apologies would be a later (and essential) development.

May it once again be said of the Church: *and there was no lonely among them.* This is withward.

Tokyo is another city that experiences high levels of transience. The lack of rootedness in that city is one of the driving factors of a high level of loneliness, which has played a significant role in Tokyo's rising suicide rate. Loneliness is so pervasive that there are now professional rent-a-friend services that attempt to stave off the feeling of isolation.[41] And in a world of competing social media, the pressure to present a life of social connection, trending popularity, and dynamic intrigue is intense. An employee for a rent-a-friend service says that many in Japan go years without being touched. She tells the story of one of her clients who cried when merely shaking hands. There are now owl cafes and cat cafes where people can go pet living animals in an effort to feel connected to something alive. That's staggering.

In a recorded conversation between the Dalai Lama and the Anglican Bishop, Desmund Tutu, the Bishop laments our current moment of increasing loneliness:

> We depend on the other in order for us to be fully who we are… The (African) concept of Ubuntu says: A person is a person through other persons. When I have a small piece of bread, it is for my benefit that I share it with you. Because, after all, none of us came into the world on our own. We needed two people to bring us into the world.[42]

Reclaiming a sense of rootedness in a location, whether you are there for 3 months or 30 years, is essential to expanding into the likeness of Jesus. We need others in our lives to accomplish this.

The second commitment for the withward direction is *intentionality*. The greatest quest in life (and consequentially the greatest challenge in our current society) is not to become more successful, or more knowledgable, or more powerful. Rather, it is to become more relational. Many people are up in arms about the threat of Artificial Intelligence becoming like humans and taking over the world. Maybe they are right. Who knows? Films and TV shows such as *Battlestar Galatica*, feature robots (Cylons) that advance to become indistinguishable next to humans. However, I don't think the real threat is robots actively becoming more human. The real threat is humans passively becoming more robotic. Radical intention toward meaningful relationships is now one of the most essential spiritual disciplines in the 21st century.

Due to forces driving increasing levels of social isolation, loneliness, and technology, we may go down as the generation that is over-connected and under-communed. We eat around each other but rarely dine with each other. I heard recently that the average American had 3 genuine friends in the early 1990s. Today that number has dwindled to 1.8. Surveys report 40 percent of Americans have no one listening to their life with them.[43] We are trending in a tragic direction. If ever there were a good moment for the Church to bear light on this present darkness, now is the time.

It was a muggy, August evening when I found myself around a peculiar dinner table in Atlanta, Georgia. I had flown south the evening before to teach at a church. My host family, Jim and Nancy, asked if I'd be willing to join their dinner group for the night. So I inquired about the nature of the group. Nancy replied, "It's ten couples that come together regularly to share a meal in our home, and we just let the conversation lead us. Our goal is to be intentional with being there for each other. The rest takes care of itself."

I sought more information, "That's cool. How long have you been meeting?" She, replied, "Uh . . . let's see, about twenty years now . . ." For twenty straight years this group had intentionally dined in one of their homes once a month. That's right. Twenty. Some of you reading this haven't been alive twenty years. That's intentional. I said, "Ok. I'm not sure I'm gonna fit in, but I'm game."

Everyone brought a dish, they opened the wine and we dined. Not grazed, dined! Jim had attended to the pulled pork for hours. The Big Green Egg took care of the rest. It was love at first bite. I mean, pulled pork, in the heart of the South. Come on! A vegetarian's nightmare. Even Ellen DeGeneres would find this meal hard to resist.

For what seemed like hours they shared common stories, laughed, and listened. And over the course of the evening the room filled with the glow of joy. Then they began recalling stories of former Christmas parties and all of the white elephant gifts. For example, inspired by the film *Christmas Vacation*, one of them had actually wrapped Aunt Bethany's jello mold with cat food on it. Around this table, in the heart of Georgia, "Dirty Santa" had never been dirtier. These people were hilariously brutal.

The reminiscing of days gone by went on and on. After two glasses of wine, and three helpings of pork, I'm laughing like an uncontrollable Middle Schooler. Then something happened. It was sudden. It was disruptive.

Nancy started weeping! Tears streaming down her face.

Everyone stopped. The silence was deafening. From the head of the table she says, "You know, it's been such a gift these past twenty years that we get to laugh around the table. But I know that when one of us loses a job, the rest of us will be right there to financially support; when our kids graduate college and enter marriage, we all will be there to celebrate; when one of us gets the diagnosis of cancer, the rest of us will drop everything and serve."

The room flooded with tears. A cocktail of finitude mixed with gratitude. There I sat. My laughter segued to awe. The Church that takes seriously the call to relationship, is the church equipped to endure any season—joy and gloom, having much and little, sickness and health.

The future of the flourishing church takes intentional relationships seriously because God takes them seriously. Many speak casually about wanting to change global society. It is quite possible that the best and only way to really accomplish change is through intention with a local community. No matter how long or short you think you will live in a given state, city, or neighborhood, the invitation of Jesus is to go deep with the people right in front of you. Chances are in twenty years they won't be there either. But in the end, your influence in them, and theirs in you will be carried into the next context of life. And that is how culture is spread. That is how the scattered, persecuted early church of the 1st century uploaded a virus of love in the Roman Empire. Withward matters.

The third commitment of the withward direction is *purpose*. I've never been able to shake *Acts 2:43-44: "Everyone was filled with awe at the many wonders and signs performed by the apostles. All the believers were together and had everything in common."*

I long for that. How does this happen? It happens as an outcome of purpose. The preceding verse reveals what the community *devoted* themselves to, which made these kinds of breakthroughs possible. They were devoted to the Scriptures, fellowship, feasting, and prayer. Simple input. Complex result. *Simplexity!*

Let's remember this narrative is descriptive, not prescriptive. Which means that these are not inputs that derive outputs. I am not suggesting if you do X, then Y will result. We are not widgets, and God is not a mechanic of the post-industrial world. I am suggesting that without a purpose one should minimize grandiose expectations. We need a shared purpose that draws us together. Instead, we are often individuals seeking to accomplish isolated dreams, drifting as islands of self-actualization. In his book, *Destroyer of the Gods*, scholar Larry Hurtado writes, "It was not down to individuals to pursue their own private improvement and development. Instead, early Christian behavioral teaching was presented as a corporate commitment and social project to which believers were summoned collectively."[44]

The early church met with purpose. Devotion to Scripture centered them on their story (notice the root of *Scripture* is *Script*). None of us can bear witness to this grand story alone. It's far too great. We all have gifts to share in building each other up and telling the story to the world.

Devotion to feasting centered them in withward spirituality. Devotion to fellowship centered them on honest conversations filled with the myriad expressions of the human experience. Devotion in prayer centered them on going upward in praise as a community. In Sebastian Junger's book, *Tribe*, he writes, "Whatever the technological advances of modern society—and they're nearly miraculous—the individualized lifestyles that those technologies spawn seem to be deeply brutalizing to the human spirit."[45] Sebastian is right. We are not to fear technology itself as a threat. We are to fear our willingness to so readily compromise our humanity. And being human centers on being relational. We learn this from a God, who in God-self, is Triune relationship. One of the ways to reclaim our likeness to God, then, is to embrace the necessity of the withward direction.

The Church, in her essence, are those peculiar people who conspire together with God for the world's renewal. The whole is greater than the sum of the parts. We are more together than apart. A renewed commitment to rootedness, intentionality, and purpose are part of what it means to reclaim our divine likeness in community. The Church matters. You matter. Withward matters.

EXPANSIVE PRACTICE _____

Remember, when Jesus taught his disciples to pray, the first word used was "Our." The entire Christian journey is based on a communal framework. Pursue someone you trust this week, and reveal something personal about your story that invites them into your journey. We are not meant to bury secrets into our souls and fake a smile. Life is hard, but is meant to be lived together in circles of trust that eventually open outward toward the world.

FIVE

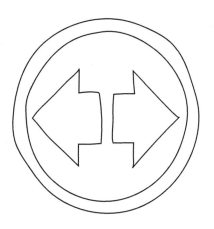

Outward

> You say you care about the poor?
> Then tell me, what are their names?
> *Gustavo Gutierrez*

Suddenly, two naked children and their mother burst from the tin house. I could see them from the balcony.

In 2005, gripped by the plight of orphans in Sierra Leone, I partnered our local church with an international orphanage organization. Determined to see the tragic scope of the situation for myself, I booked a flight. For a week I lived in a mud hut with an incredible tribe, deep in the bush. Those were some of the best days of my life. I spent my waking hours walking from village to village, channeling questions through my translator about life, food, family, and spirituality. In the evenings I read books by candlelight, dining on power bars and canned tuna within the confines of my little hut. The bathing "situation" was unforgettable. Configured like an outhouse without a roof, the shower was housed in a tin, rectangular structure. A humble boy in the village would serve me buckets of water, warmed by fireside, to pour over my body. Dripping wet, I looked up into the midnight sky. The Milky Way stared straight back at me. I thought to myself, "This is what it feels like to be essentially human." No cell phone, no electricity, no emails, no schedule, just night sky, and bright stars, and warm water, and the sound of crickets. Thousands and thousands of crickets.

Upon my return to the nation's capital, the organization put me up in the guesthouse to sleep before catching my flight home. It was there that the harsh realities of everyday life punched me in the gut. Returning from a hike, I rested in thought on the third-level balcony. The morning sun was scorching. The bottled water was refreshing. The Atlantic Ocean rolled in the distance. The view of the city was serene. The persistent soundtrack of generators, pumping cool air against me in contrast with the warm climate was sublime. Shifting my gaze from the horizon to the ground, everything changed.

Next to the guesthouse was a tin shed. It looked like nothing more than a storage closet for some rakes and shovels, and one could possibly fit a wheelbarrow inside the structure. A makeshift door opened and, unexpectedly, out popped two children and their mother. From the shed the mother retrieved a small suitcase that contained what looked like a couple of dirty shirts and some tattered pants. Dressing them both it occurred to me that the suitcase was their closet and the shed was their home. I cried.

I was reminded of a sentence that author, Donald Miller, once uttered: *Other people exist.*[46]

I was about to board a flight and without a plan of return. Landing in Orlando International Airport, I'd retrieve my car, pay my parking fee, drive to my home, turn on my lights, open my fridge, grab a cold beverage, adjust the thermostat, shower at the turn of a knob, climb into bed, and sleep off the jet-lag. Meanwhile, half a world away this woman would do the same thing the next day she had done the previous: open the suitcase and select one of two dirty shirts her children would wear that day. I'd soon forget her and get on with my distracted post-industrial life.

For billions of people everyday, life is really hard.

One of the virtues most needed today is holy empathy. It's the willingness to see others in their plight, care deeply, and respond with compassion. We are all connected. The well being of Sierra Leone should mean something to the well being of the United States. The well being of that woman and her children means something to my own well being. I am not whole unless she is whole.

How then do we permit these convicting moments to impress a permanent lifestyle into us? How can this one moment from a balcony change everything about the way I see life and my role in this world? This is the essence of the outward direction. Other people exist!

Just then a lawyer stood up to test Jesus. 'Teacher,' he said, 'what must I do to inherit eternal life?' He said to him, 'What is written in the law? What do you read there?' He answered, 'You shall love the Lord your God with all your heart, and with all your soul, and with all your strength, and with all your mind; and your neighbor as yourself.' And he said to him, 'You have given the right answer; do this, and you will live.'

But wanting to justify himself, he asked Jesus, 'And who is my neighbor?' Jesus replied, 'A man was going down from Jerusalem to Jericho, and fell into the hands of robbers, who stripped him, beat him, and went away, leaving him half dead. Now by chance a priest was going down that road; and when he saw him, he passed by on the other side. So likewise a Levite, when he came to the place and saw him, passed by on the other side. But a Samaritan while traveling came near him; and when he saw him, he was moved with pity. He went to him and bandaged his wounds, having poured oil and wine on them. Then he put him on his own animal, brought him to an inn, and took care of him. The next day he took out two denarii, gave them to the innkeeper, and said, "Take care of him; and when I come back, I will repay you whatever more you spend." Which of these three, do you think, was a neighbor to the man who fell into the hands of the robbers?' He said, 'The one who showed him mercy.' Jesus said to him, 'Go and do likewise.' (Luke 10:25-37 NRSV)

Jesus told stories—lots and lots of stories. Stories help us re-imagine what tends to become familiar. By subtle changes in the characters' backgrounds, genders, ethnicities, and so forth, stories aid us in expanding our worldview. This happened with King David when confronted by Nathan about an unjust situation where a wealthy man with many sheep took the one and only sheep of a poor man to prepare it for a feast. When David heard the fiction he was angry and rebuked the rich man for his action. Through story Nathan rebukes David's murderous action toward Uriah, the late husband of Bathsheba. When we imagine ourselves in a narrative, it can disrupt over-familiarity. Jesus was a master storyteller.

This was a hard story for the lawyer. It went against the grain of every listener eavesdropping. Not only does Jesus expand his worldview of "neighbor," but, his socio-religious nemesis, a Samaritan, becomes the hero. How disruptive! Jesus was essentially dismantling the lawyer's tribal, insular, self-righteous, self-seeking, group-think worldview. This is not so dissimilar to what the Spirit would seek to do in our time.

The point of utilizing this story begs a couple of questions: Is expansion in your worldview possible? Is the expansion of your worldview crucial? The stories Jesus told often stretch our points of view to reconsider people we might otherwise omit. But our human tendency is to seek others who remind us of ourselves. There is a cognitive explanation for this that I will detail below. Suffice it to say, it can be a real struggle in a fast-paced world to dignify our differences.

EXPANSIVE IDEA

Many find it easy to open their tables, their homes, and their lives to others, yet do so exclusively toward those with whom they share a similar income bracket, education level, and cultural background. But the nature of biblical hospitality—the nature of the Kingdom—is inconvenience and diversity.

Consider this: God became human. How inconvenient! Never before has a living entity experienced greater diversity than the eternal, second person of the Trinity, becoming a finite, Jewish human being. God comprehends inconvenience and diversity at a visceral level. God taking human flesh modeled the way for an outwardly-oriented life. Convenient living and the Kingdom of God are not typically compatible. Other people exist.

There is something to be said about the misers, the widgets, and the cosmos.

Back in the 1980s—the best decade for music if I might say so—social psychologists coined the term *cognitive miser*. I first learned of this term from Christina Cleveland's work, *Disunity in Christ*.[47] It means that humans naturally tend to conserve mental energy. The human brain is incredible. But the human brain is limited. Its ability to process information is staggering. Yet in the age of 24-hour news coverage, addictions to smart phones, raising kids, taking tests, incessant text messaging, and pervasive social media . . . our brains are tired.

So, here is what we do: We naturally use mental shortcuts to conserve brain energy, hence, cognitive miser. This means our brains create categories to dump info into . . . and our brains are subject to error. Let's return to the Good Samaritan story. I suggest that the lawyer most likely has a worldview that goes something like: all Samaritans are the same. They are religious imposters of the true Israel, who worship in a false place, and couldn't possibly be right in the eyes of God.

As previously stated, it was inconceivable that the Samaritan would be a character in Jesus' story, and would then turn out to be the actual hero over and above the priest or Levite. It would be one thing if the priest summoned the energy to help a defenseless Samaritan who had been robbed. But that is not the full extent of the worldview Jesus wants to disrupt. Jesus presents a tale where the Samaritan, the imposter, saves the day! This is a Kyser Sosay, *The Usual Suspects*, turn of events. I'm assuming Jesus just dropped the microphone and walked away slowly as his listeners gasped for air.

We are cognitive misers. We lazily categorize people into shapes and sizes that do injustice to their full humanity. We do this because our brains need to make sense out of this complex world and because they are tired. We need an expansion of worldview.

That brings us to widgets. We are prone to see others, particularly those who are "not like us," as widgets. I first stumbled across the term when studying business marketing in my undergrad education. Widget is a business term applied generally to products across the board. It's a shorthand way of homogenizing, categorizing. Widgets are a term utilized to simplify complexity. But it strips every product of its given uniqueness.

To be fair, categories can be really helpful. Animals are classified into species, history into eras, politics into the colors red and blue. These generalities can give us access to data on a meta level. In an age where information is constantly streaming, we have to form categories for the sake of sanity. But categories have drawbacks. When applying the concept of widgets to people, which is easy to do, stereotypes emerge, people are batched into groups, and are then discarded as less than individuals with their own unique stories. In other words, just because you see the color of another person's skin, does not mean you know that person in the slightest.

It often plays out like this:

Another black life taken,

Another blue officer down,

Another Muslim radicalized,

Another immigrant recruited by a drug cartel.

And the cognitive miser within seduces us to widget the world:

All black lives are suspicious,

All blue officers are racist,

All Muslims are terrorists,

All immigrants are deviants.

This is beyond disappointing. This is tragic. Compounding the effect of cognitive miser, the widget worldview causes us to generalize, and thus *dehumanize*.

Over time we begin to relate exclusively to people around us who share non-essential similarities (such as skin color, income bracket, education level, or even less significant, people who like the same televisions shows, or essentials oils, or people who eat sushi). We think, "You eat rainbow roll too! OMG, we must be soul mates!" Facing inward toward those who reinforce our superficial preferences, we demonize those we perceive are different or who disagree with our opinions. In an interview, the Dalai Lama talks about the long-term health consequences of sacralizing personal preference:

> Too much focus on yourself leads to stress and high blood pressure. Many years ago, I was at a gathering of medical scientists and researchers in New York. One of the medical scientists said in his presentation that those people who disproportionately use the first-person pronouns—I, I, I, me, me, me, and mine, mine, mine—have a significantly greater risk of having a heart attack. With too much self-focus your vision becomes narrow, and with this even a small problem appears out of proportion and unbearable.[48]

Essentially, the same can be said about surrounding ourselves only with people that reinforce our preferences, personalities, and opinions. To live in this way is to reject the outward way of Jesus.

In the same interview, Bishop Desmund Tutu agreed, adding the African concept of *Ubuntu* to the conversation:

> We are wired to be caring for the other and generous to one another. We shrivel when we are not able to interact. I mean that is part of the reason why solitary confinement is such a horrendous punishment. We depend on the other in order for us to be fully who we are . . . [A] concept that we have at home, *Ubuntu*, says: A person is a person through other

persons. Ubuntu says when I have a small piece of bread, it is for my benefit that I share it with you. Because, after all, none of us came into the world on our own. We needed two people to bring us into the world.[49]

This argument is useful for both the withward and outward directions. We need community, but we also need community with others who invite us into a deeper, more diverse human experience. We become more fully who we are through contact, communication, and communion with other people!

Let's think about it politically. In 1994, the majority of Americans were either conservative moderates, or liberal moderates. That moment has passed. Fast-forward twenty years to 2014 and data suggests the majority of Americans are trending far right or far left, hollowing out the middle. This middle is where compromise can take place for the sake of advancing the whole. What we are left with is a society of ideology. This leads to cultural gridlock, which spawns all sorts of societal maladies where compromise is no longer a viable way forward. Many today are so over-identified with extreme groupthink that they think it repulsive to, and cannot co-exist with others who disagree with them. Humility, civility, and empathy are imperative ingredients to rehumanize a culture of difference. Sometimes our *postures* toward others matter more than the positions we hold. We can (and should) hold *positions* on all varieties of ethics. But when we fail to hold a posture of humility within those positions, dehumanization can quickly surface.

An obstacle to pursuing the outward direction is our human tendency to exclusively surround ourselves with people who remind us of ourselves. This tendency keeps us ignorant in our assessments of others.

Better than any organization in the world, the Church is equipped to end racism, sexism, and bigotry. This is because the Holy Spirit, who raised Jesus from the dead and was sent to indwell the

Church, empowers her. But we often cower, following patterns of the world of widgets rather than the courageous, outward way of Jesus: understanding that to dignify all people as image bearers of God, and then seeking to rehumanize the world is not synonymous with affirming unbiblical lifestyles of unbridled desire. We can affirm another's dignity, while not endorsing their actions. To live into the outward direction means we must reclaim human dignity as our primal instinct. This seems to be the pattern of Jesus. Other people exist.

There is a phrase in my soul I cannot shake. And I'm not sure I'm supposed to: "*Follow the cosmos.*" Many physicists are now theorizing that the universe is infinitely expanding. Perhaps this spatial expansion reflects the design of God's relentless love. This is evidenced most clearly by the Word made flesh. Again, this is not the same as endorsing every ethic and behavior as equally virtuous and true. It does, however, mean that our first response toward the world is openness to the humanity of others, despite our differences. From this place, empathy can flow. When we do this, we reenact to others the expansive love God offers us in Jesus.

In sum, our human limitations default to contracting our humanity rather than expanding us outward. This has been true since Genesis 3. Jesus came to reverse this trend. Conserving energy, our brains act as misers. This lazy maneuver turns others into widgets as we generalize, stereotype, and categorize in an effort to make sense of incessant information. The call of Jesus is to resist generalization that leads to dehumanization. The Kingdom demands we see individuals and seek to hear their stories before forming opinions. This is what Jesus did when the woman caught in the act of adultery was brought to him (John 8:1-11). He identified first with her humanity, then, later addressed her behavior. This same truth is what Jesus teaches us in the story of the Good Samaritan. But it begs the question, if God is calling us outward, to see the world renewed, then where is God? If we are called to participate in this holy work to value the other and rehumanize the world, why does this God often seem distant, absent even? I think J.R.R. Tolkien was asking these same kinds of questions when writing his famous fiction, *The Lord of the Rings: "Where is Gandalf?"*

The Christian story asserts that God is headed somewhere with the world. And despite the past and present dehumanizing policies, partisan politics, and temporal power structures, Jesus' eternal Kingship will eventually be made known in all of the earth. His reign will renew all of creation and bring about flourishing to those who seek to join him. This is not a distant vision only; it's a present in-breaking. Participating with God toward this end is what gives us hope to press on in the face of despair. Tolkien's image of Gandalf hints at this notion of God's renewal. But at least half of the book the reader is left to wonder, "Where is Gandalf?" Did he really die on the bridge fighting the Balrog of Moria? Like, die die? The reader hopes that Gandalf is alive somewhere, out of sight, and doing really important work. But when Frodo needs him most, Gandalf seems distant, absent, or disinterested. Or maybe he really is dead.

"Where is Gandalf!?" This is kind of what I hear a lot from Christians today.

Where is God?

Does God exist?

Does God really love creation?

Then why so much pain?

Why the sorrow and mourning and tears and terror and cancer and death?

These are sensible questions, particularly in light of a God whom, we believe is love. What I think Gandalf has to teach us is that the end is worth the wait. And in the wait we are called to participate toward that same end because our participation brings about transformation within ourselves and in the world around us. Our lives tell a similar story to that of Frodo Baggins—a diminutive hobbit who wrestled wildly with insecurity and self-preservation. By the end of his transformative journey Frodo realizes that he cannot return home to the way he used to live. He is a changed hobbit. His former vision of self-preservation, surrounding himself with hobbits who reinforce his preferences, is just too small. Somewhere along the journey of life his former worldview was forever disrupted.

The meaning of Frodo's journey is best summarized in a sermon by Dr. Martin Luther King, Jr.: "The belief that God will do everything for man is as untenable as the belief that man can do everything for himself . . . we must learn that to expect God to do everything while we do nothing is not faith but superstition."[50] Ours is a faith of participation. Faith is not merely cognitive assertions we hold in our heads. Faith is a decision to jump into a particular stream of action based on where we hope the story is headed. Christians have been given a "revelation" of where all things are headed. The woman of faith is the one who begins rehearsing wholeness toward a broken world. The man of faith is the one who turns outward in love toward the neighbor, the stranger and, yes, even a Samaritan enemy.

In the story of the Good Samaritan, Jesus is saying to the lawyer, if you want eternal life you must become like God, and permit the expansion of your capacity to love. It is there that transformation becomes possible—for you, the other, and the entire world. May you stretch into Christlikeness as you intentionally serve someone outside of your comfort zone. The Kingdom life is often inconvenient. Like the cosmos, the Kingdom is expansive, and so are you.

EXPANSIVE PRACTICE ———————————————

Start small. The Samaritan was the enemy for the lawyer. Who is your enemy? Would you permit God to expand your worldview by spending time each day this week praying for your enemy and writing letters to them in a journal? At the conclusion of the week would you consider doing some small act of faith toward your enemy that enacts where the world is headed in Jesus' name? If nothing comes to mind, would you simply bless your enemy and ask the love of God to embrace them and give them peace?

SIX

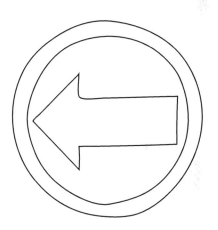

Backward

> Tradition is not to preserve the ashes,
> but to pass on the flame.
> *Gustav Mahler*

It was the year 2000. The anxiety of Y2K came and went. The cost of gas was a manageable $1.26 per gallon. A lesser-known fact in the world, I graduated high school . . . barely. And in the midst of all that, in the wonderful world of film, the year 2000 was nothing short of spectacular.

Gladiator ("are you not entertained?!"), *Snatch*, *The Patriot*, and *The Family Man*—all in the same year. We were spoiled. Remember *Cast Away*? In a spectacular year for film, it was an outlier. Cast Away was the movie that would never end. And then it did. And we all went home grateful it was over, vowing never to speak of it again. If you never saw it, congratulations. The list goes on. *Remember the Titans*, *Gone in 60 Seconds* (a productive year for Nick Cage), the preposterous motorcycle fight scene in *Mission Impossible 2*, and the unforgettable classic, *Meet the Parents*. As compelling as many of these films are, none deserve the opening story of this chapter. The story belongs to, what I see, as the most underrated film of the year 2000: *Memento*. And to that film we now turn our attention.

Essentially Memento tells the tale of a man attempting to avenge the homicide of his girlfriend. But due to an injury to his head, he suffers from short-term memory loss, a condition known as anterograde amnesia. He sets out to conduct his own investigation, taking notes and snapping polaroids because he's lost the capacity to store new memories—it's literally a total head trip.

Maybe you're thinking: *Whoa! Spoiler alert...*

My reply: *Settle down!*

Memento was released years ago. If you haven't seen it by now pause here and go watch it. At the end of the film the main character solves the mystery: the murderer . . . is . . . him. That's embarrassing.

For the purpose of the backward direction, this film matters because it captures the essence of memory. Going backward plays a greater significance in everyday life than many realize. Anyone with a friend or family member suffering from dementia or Alzheimer's will confirm that claim. Mental impairment is tragic because the inability to form new memories and recall old ones disconnects us from the continuity of life. Memory matters. Kierkegaard was right: "We live life forward, but we understand it backward." If that is true, it may also be true that, due to our preoccupation with the future, we do not understand our lives very much in the contemporary moment. We are like spiritual amnesiacs.

In the spring of 2013 I met a new friend named Ed Gungor. He was hosting a conference in Oklahoma and invited me to play a small part in it. I caught a flight from NYC (where I was pastoring at the time) to Tulsa. It was my first opportunity to both teach and learn from Pentecostals. Having no previous experience with that tradition, I was confused as to what I might possibly contribute. To my surprise, Ed revealed the theme: "historic Christianity."

Yeah. It stunned me too.

He was seeking to curate a conference for pastors who were hungry to, as he called it, "resource tradition." This was particularly intriguing for me given how much time is spent in the contemporary church either resisting or running from any and every tradition. To be fair, the Church is gorged with sins from her past. From crusades, to slavery, to moral/social/fiduciary corruption, to sexual and emotional abuse, the history of the Church isn't exactly a spotless lamb. However, there is no other movement in the history of the world that has spawned so much good in the face of systemic evil. From the creation of hospitals, to orphan and widow care, to charities formed in Jesus' name, there is a great deal of wheat historically sown among the weeds. We have much to resource from the ones who came before us, upon whose shoulders we stand.

I returned home from the conference with a ridiculous idea: to teach a Church history course on a weekday evening in a local Manhattan church. I began wondering whether there were others craving a spiritual depth accessible by digging into the past? And whether the barrier wasn't the content of history, but the packaging of that history in a compelling, accessible, and practical format. Better put: How might a local church rethink presenting the riches of our past in a way that was engaging and meaningful? *That* is what I set out to do.

So in the peak of summer in New York City—the time of year when most people travel, become even more non-committal, and aspire to use their brains as little as possible—I launched my first history course in the local parish. Anticipating a handful of history nuts with some extra time on their hands, I was stunned to find the class full to capacity with Gen-Xers and Millenials, determined to learn about martyrs, early Christian practices, and Desert Fathers in order to deepen their formation into the likeness of Jesus.

What was happening?

I believe we are beginning to witness a remnant of serious Christians weary from being so easily seduced by novelty, entertainment, and self-preoccupation. Observing Americans in the 19th century, Alexis De Tocqueville said, "Each citizen is habitually engaged in the contemplation of a very puny object, namely himself."[51] And that was before the days of selfies! Ours is a cultural moment where we must not only resist the trend toward biblical illiteracy, but historical illiteracy as well. Underneath the pursuit of our spiritual ancestry lies a well deep enough to slake the thirst of anyone seeking, in the words of Nietzsche, "A long obedience in the same direction."[52] What is happening is better visualized than expressed. Recently I was hiking in Los Angeles' Griffith Park. The roots of the tree above capture the essence of what I hope is happening in our time.

EXPANSIVE IDEA

In a subconscious quest for deep Christianity, many are reaching for a faith far beyond fog machines, slogans, and series graphics. The roots of our souls are stretching to find soil that is substantive.

The question is whether the local church is willing to cultivate contexts where depth can become possible, where formation can take place. The soul's depth is what the backward direction primarily contributes toward our pursuit of Christlikeness. In a faith asking questions beyond "How do I get to heaven," this direction helps advance the cause to pursue the Kingdom on earth.

SCRIPTURE

Look to the Lord and his strength; seek his face always.

Remember the wonders he has done,

his miracles, and the judgments he pronounced (Psalm 105:4-5 NIV)

Let this passage linger. Perhaps re-read it. It may be more profound than you think. Once, while meditating on this text at morning prayer, I was struck by the connection between the past and the present. For example, notice how verse 4 is devoted to seeking God in the present moment. The Psalmist's greatest aim in life is to find God in *the now*, the present moment. But notice how the writer suggests accomplishing this: by remembering the past. There is something mysterious about the past that we are meant to import into the present. Remembering God's activity in past activity somehow opens us to receive God's activity in the present. It is accessed through faith. Faith is built through hearing stories of God's faithfulness, remembering the wonders done in ages gone by, and seeking a fresh outpouring based on how God has manifested in times past. It's not so much that God does *new* (novel) things, but more that God does *fresh* things. The God who revealed is the God who reveals; the God who created is the God who creates; the God who acted is the God who acts. Past meets present. And when that happens our present can point us toward a hopeful future. Truly, those who drink deeply from the past are best equipped to live powerfully toward the future.

If ever in Israel at the right time, I highly recommend attending a Passover Seder. As Jewish people re-narrate their lives by retelling the story of the Exodus, a strange mysticism emerges that only a focused ear will pick up on. When retelling the story, they use the pronoun "we" instead of "they." Many Jews audaciously believe to be presently connected to what happened in the past. Plainly put, the Jews identify themselves as conversant with their dead ancestors, who, for them, may not be as dead as some imagine. Somehow the past becomes mysteriously present when retelling the story. The notion that somehow God, through faith, is "re-presented" in the present from events in the past is foreign to our modern sensibilities. Our backward direction then isn't merely looking back to the past for some inspiration. It's a retelling of the past, through the power of the Spirit, in hopes that the same God who moved then will once again move now. Which makes me wonder: maybe time isn't merely chronological.

Consider the prophet Amos. Hundreds of years after the Red Sea event, in which the Israelites escaped the tyranny of Pharaoh, the prophet writes:

Thus says the Lord . . .

'I brought you up out of the land of Egypt,

and led you for forty years in the wilderness,

to possess the land of the Amorite.' (Amos 2:6,10)

Although the event was definitely in the rearview mirror, Amos writes of the account as if it happened to those living in the present. There is a kind of historical-existential continuity in genuine spirituality. Not only have we received a faith that was first given to our ancestors, but we are mysteriously tethered to them in such a way that their stories become our stories, their faith becomes our faith, their lives are interwoven with our lives. We stand not alone, but on shoulders. Surely this is what the writer of Hebrews was getting at when writing on the "cloud of witnesses" who relentlessly cheer us on. Apparently they "surround us" (Hebrews 12). One is unwise, then, to pursue novelty over faithfulness. Not only is novelty fleeting, but, it's powerless. This is why the writer of 2 Timothy challenges the reader to discern between historic truth and novel trends; that days will come when itching ears are dissatisfied with only wanting to hear the latest philosophy to market. In her seminal work, *Crucifixion*, Fleming Rutledge picks up on this theme, stating:

> The old story about the fathers and mothers become the new story for the generation just emerging, who become actors in the story as their parents and grandparents did before them. If the tale remains simply a stirring narrative about a past episode, however 'inspirational,' then it is not the life-transforming story that ancient Israel knew it to be.[53]

Rutledge affirms that we join a hall of faith, of living witnesses who challenge us to bring times past into times present. When the writer of Exodus calls the Israelites to mark the Passover as a memorial day (Exodus 12:14,17), remembering means bringing the past forward into the present. This is precisely what the Apostle Paul is getting at in 1 Corinthians 11 pertaining to the new Passover in the death of Jesus. We somehow mysteriously summon that historic moment from Golgotha into our present Eucharist. Weekly Eucharist is a dynamic encounter more than it is a backward glance. The Spirit of God takes what happened in the past and brings it powerfully forward to meet us in the present. This is accessed through faith, where Christ is present.

SCAFFOLDING

Depth > Back

Framing our thoughts matters. How we frame the pursuit of the backward direction will determine our level of commitment and inspiration to do the hard work necessary to learn. Without proper vision of why history matters, most will inevitably veer toward entertainment at the end of the day. Backward is not so much about reading/learning "back into time" as much as descending "down into depth." Think of it like roots in soil. It is about rooting ourselves into something deeper, something that both includes and transcends time. Our understanding of the past can anchor us in a depth to provide clarity for where we are going. The backward direction plunges us into a depth beyond ourselves. It allows us to cultivate root systems that resource when experiencing the darkest storms of life.

In our first year of marriage, Elaina and I went through two incredible storms in the same season (maybe you're there right now, hanging onto the last thread of your faith). We were planting a church in California while her father was battling terminal cancer in Georgia. His days were numbered; her days were darkened. Meanwhile my parents in Florida were divorcing. Their marriage was ending; my days were darkened. It was hard, particularly three time zones away. Our faith was challenged immensely during that season. It became clear to me that my faith was rooted in little more than a string of cheap slogans, ephemeral worship songs, and spontaneous prayer. My non-denominational, contemporary church, relevant, jean-wearing, hipster-looking, progressive-seeking sensibilities failed to provide for me the depth necessary to weather the storm. I began wondering: Are there deeper pools of faith in which to swim? Because whatever got me to this moment is inadequate to sustain my faith journey and lead me into greater Christ-likeness.

I wanted a faith that was deeper than most of the songs you hear on Christian radio, which by and large alter our moods rather than heal our souls. I wanted a faith that swam in the streams from the past that could buoy my faith through divorce, and cancer, and vocational disappointment. I wanted a historic Christianity from which to resource tradition that I may hold the joys along with the sorrows, and the laughter along with the pain.

And thus began my quest for depth:

Saturday mornings at Torah study in the local Reformed Synagogue.

Evening readings of the Eastern Orthodox Christians.

Morning meanderings with the Medieval Mystics.

Lunch time prayers with the Catholic Saints.

Systematics in Seminary with the Calvinists.

Dining with the advocates of Social Justice.

Worshiping at conferences with the Charismatics.

And years later living with the Episcopalians in New York City.

I don't know a lot. But I know this: Christianity is beautifully diverse and incredibly deep. The same Jesus who is readily accessible to a child, can also become utterly mysterious to an elder.

Christianity is worth your life. And the Church stands on thousands of years of history to teach us. In the words of my friend, Sarah Bessey: "May we be ecclesiastically promiscuous." So when we talk about looking backward, we mean we seek to be a community who roots in an ancient path.

What + Why

Maybe you are saying to yourself: "I tried tradition, AJ. It's dead. Let's move on." My response would be that most who feel this way are given the "what" of tradition, but rarely the "why." Overwhelmed with "do this, don't do that," "go here, don't go there," church for you was a weekly experience where the goal was simply to endure. Let me illustrate this through imagery. Consider the cartoon below:[54]

This image resonates with many ex-Christians who grew up in traditions where the stories told were no longer being faithfully lived by the ones telling them. In other words, the past was severed from the present. Perhaps there was little to no anticipation of God doing things fresh in their time. So the call was simply to show up, hear the story, pray the prayer, sing the song, endure the preaching, occasionally eat the wafer, and then get back to life as usual. Notice in the cartoon that the parents are handing the faith down to the child in a written document rather than embodying the story. Christianity is meant to be an embodied faith that retells the story that we, ourselves, are attempting to live in a long line of ancestral continuity. When the pursuit of the Living God is exchanged for mere lessons of another age, the next generation interprets that what was once alive is now dead. This is terrible. It is understandable why so many are leaving church. When the "what" becomes a lecture and the "why" is lost, vitality has left the building.

Now consider this image, a sculpture by American artist, Victor Issa, from Meijer Gardens in Grand Rapids, Michigan.

As the grandfather passes on the story to his grandchild, you can see the wonder in his eyes, the passion in his hands, the sincerity in his smile. What he is passing on is clearly not just another story on another day. Rather, he's passing on a firm conviction living deeply within him. Psalm 105:5 immediately sprang to mind when I first saw the sculpture: "Remember the wonders he has done!" And let us never forget Psalm 78:6: "So the next generation would know (your teachings), even the children yet to be born." In the compelling wisdom of composer, Gustav Mahler, "Tradition is not to pass on the ashes, but to preserve the flame." The Church needs storytellers who believe the story, who live the story, and are willing to tell the story. Historically this is called evangelism. Evangelism happens when a follower of Jesus experiences God in the present, based on the story of the past, with a conviction about the future. We must not only tell the "what" of Christianity but also be convinced of "why" the faith matters in the first place.

Joy - Pain

I meet many well-intentioned, good-mannered people who consider themselves "de-churched." They are the new "nones." They are not monolithic, but diverse. Some left religion behind due to abuses in their respected faiths. Others left due to being overwhelmed by the "what" of religion without ever hearing the "why" underneath it. However, the most utilized motivation for people leaving church is due to that pesky gap between their expectations and their experience. That gap is also known as disappointment. Many former Christians simply do not have a theology that has space for pain. And they are disappointed. Joys are welcomed, but pain is despised. So when pain is experienced, many of them are sadly told (by pastors no less) that something must be wrong with *them*. Again, this is terrible. Another reason for this loss of faith when pain arrives is a contemporary church culture where songs must always be upbeat, rhyme, and sound like the ditties you'd hear on mainstream radio. In this kind of church culture, seasons like Lent are omitted, and Easter Sunday is fast-tracked. But who are we kidding? The incessant headlines of 24-hour news cycles remind us just how broken the world is. So our quest for joy minus pain is disrupted every time we turn on the local news.

While experiencing that difficult season in California, I had another breakthrough of faith while going backward. As I read about the saints, the martyrs, and the desert fathers, I found a rolodex of spiritual ancestors who were just as, if not, more tormented than me. Yet, the common denominator with all of these people is that they finished their spiritual race. If they, who lived in far greater need, persecution, and disease than we in the 21st century West, were able to keep the faith, why are we so fickle? What are we missing? An understanding of the already/not yet Kingdom for one thing. An understanding of the past for another. For the purpose of this chapter, we will focus on the latter.

EXPANSIVE IDEA

The martyrs built their faith upon the promise of another Kingdom. These early Christians lived so radically for Jesus they considered it a joy to die for Him. Yet I frequently experience Christians leaving contemporary churches in droves because they don't have a category for pain.

They believe they are alone, and that the sorrows of the earth are unique to their time period. This is the fruit of an individualistic, self-infatuated society, which has pervaded the Western Church. When people walk away from faith, it's sometimes because the Church has ill-equipped them to understand the paradoxical tension between the goodness of God, the future Kingdom come, and the present reality of pain. And this is where Church history can work its magic. The faithful lives of the saints can help us reframe our momentary pains into a larger context of ultimate renewal.

Hear the reframing of Peter as he equips the early Church: "Do not be surprised at the fiery ordeal that has come on you . . . as though something strange were happening" (1 Peter 4:12). The resource of Church history situates us in a long lineage of persecution, poverty, and pain. This doesn't mean that we will not experience foretastes of the future resurrection (see Forward chapter).

But it does awaken us to the cloud of witnesses who cheer us on from past ages, inspiring us to finish the race because every cross we bear eventually finds its end in resurrection. Tragically, many today remain largely ignorant to our spiritual ancestors because we strive to be forward-thinking, progressives who are entitled to immediacy! To these I would counsel that the best and deepest journey toward the future is always tethered to the past.

Our history doesn't take us backward in time as much as it takes us downward in depth. It roots us in the faith, reminding us to reclaim the "why" along with the "what," to finally make space for the pain of this world to situate alongside the joy—knowing the story finds its fulfillment in Jesus making all things new.

A final story. My friend is a Bishop in a stream of the Episcopal Church. He tells of a time when, swinging his six year-old granddaughter in the backyard, she made a passing comment that spoke to him on deeper levels. Grinning from ear to ear she says, "Grandpa, if I pull backward really hard, and then kick forward really far, I can go really high!" He replied, "That's right, sweetie. That's right."

Mysteriously, to soar into new heights means digging deep into the past. The past is meant to be brought into our present, and our present relies on a God who is not only with us now, but waiting for us in the future. This is the direction we call *forward*, and to that direction belongs the next chapter.

EXPANSIVE PRACTICE _____

One of the reasons we flee the backward direction is because it can feel exhaustive. Where do we begin digging into our long and storied past? This is true not only with Church history, but all genres of history. All too often, studying history feels like acquiring tidbits of minutiae that are difficult to fit within a larger whole. It's overwhelming—like someone throwing a fist full of sand toward you and asking you to catch. Therefore, I have found that learning of the historical time periods of history is far easier and more compelling. This comes to us in the form of major movements such as the martyrs, the monks, the reformers, the missionaries, etc. Consider starting with Gerald Sittser's book, *Water From a Deep Well*. He narrows (without cheapening) Church history into twelve major movements, and then provides essential narrative content. If you follow the footnotes, you can dig further into any of the major movements as you feel drawn.

To be sure, many Christians throughout time have flourished without having access to the wide swath of history available in ours. However, within a culture embedded with messages of novelty, autonomy, and self-preoccupation, it may be that the depths we are searching for are not discovered in the pursuit of self-actualization and contemporary relevance as much as a deeper awareness of our past, lending us a greater vision toward our future.

SEVEN

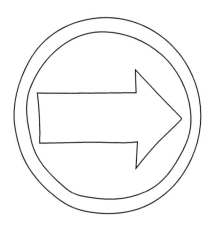

Forward

The end is where we start from.
T.S. Eliot

There's odd, there's weird, and then there's Erica. She is a category unto herself. A healer if I ever met one. Whenever I think of her, I think of pick-up basketball. One of the prerequisites to any serious game of pick-up is someone on the court who can't play worth a lick, but rounds out the group of ten. Inevitably that person is last picked. The team lowers all expectation placed upon him, and, at best, hopes for some solid defense. Now, the last thing you want him doing is summoning the confidence to shoot the basketball. Yet I have found, more often than not, he rarely has the self-awareness to simply pass the ball and not shoot. In fact, sometimes he has so much confidence that he shoots every time he gets the ball. It's really awkward. And then, 30 feet away from the basket, the unexpected happens.

Aligning his shoulder with the basket, he goes into his motion. I utter inaudibly, "Don't shoot!" The probability of his 30-foot 3-pointer going in is about as low as the Republicans and Democrats coming together on any policy in the 21st century. But shoot he does. And to my surprise, it banks off the backboard and into the basket. On the way down the court I extend my hand for a high five—which he clumsily misses—and say, "Great shot. I was with you all of the way." This metaphor is an accurate way of describing my time with Erica.

I'm not sure she has ever touched a basketball, but she's touched a lot of people in her life. Several years ago while living in California, she came to visit Elaina and me. We lived in an area that was about as hostile to Christianity as any I've experienced—spiritual, not religious types. Which, in America, usually means: I'm open to anything but Christianity, and I'm definitely not interested in the local church. On a Saturday afternoon we strolled into Rite Aid for some reason or another. Erica—weird Erica—notices a woman in a wheelchair. I walk by her thinking nothing at all. Elaina walks by her praying, "Lord have mercy."

Erica walks to her and stops. Here it comes. Things are about to get awkward. Rite Aid has no idea that a healer just walked into the storefront carrying no fear of man. I'm all of the way down the aisle by the time I notice that Erica hadn't followed the leader—namely, me. She detoured, following a better leader—namely, Jesus. Elaina and I knew what was about to go down. I leaned in and whispered, "This kind of stuff might work back where Erica's from, but there is no way Long Beach will go for this." It was the spiritual equivalent to a 30-foot 3-pointer. It might as well have been a 300-footer. I could feel the tension rising up in my throat.

Erica quickly connects with this women, receives permission to pray, and seconds later the woman stands up in the middle of Rite Aid on Aisle 3. It was weird. It was incredible. And at that moment within my chest I said to God: "If you're doing this, I want in."

I was weary of living a faith that was bound to my reason. I like reason. It's just that if God is only capable of performing that which I can reason, I will inevitably reduce God to my size. The Scripture seems to be, among many things, a collection of narratives where God is constantly challenging humans to permit the expansion of their worldview. Christianity is a faith of surprise. Moses on the mountain—surprise. David as a King—surprise. Mary as pregnant—surprise. Those 12 disciples—surprise. Jesus is Risen—surprise. Someone once said, the mind is a wonderful servant, but a terrible master. I think that's true.

This is forward. It is awkward. But it is incredible. An unlikely 30-foot swish—surprise.

For God so loved the world that he gave his one and only Son, that who-ever believes in him shall not perish but have eternal life. (John 3:16 NIV)

It's one thing to have theories and stories. It's another to find scriptural support for your theories and stories. Beyond both of these it's best to permit Scripture to drive our theories and stories. Familiarity can serve both as an incredible gift and an unhelpful burden. In an age seduced by novelty, we often prevent the Scriptures from *knowing us* because we assume we *know them* so well. I invite you to reconsider your familiarity with John 3:16. Resist the notion that you know everything there is to consider with this passage. We see this Scripture everywhere: Sunday School, football games, protests, street evangelists, and so forth. Truthfully, many are tired of it, submerging it in a sea of familiarity. Even worse, we perceive the people who proclaim it most often live it least.

I was raised to assume this Scripture was entirely about a future moment. Future? Yes. Entirely? No. The notion was to pray a prayer of salvation in the present that will secure your eternity in the future. I'm not arguing that there is not some truth to that. I'm arguing this is not the whole story. There is more truth to extract from this phenomenally familiar text. Textual reduction is such a waste.

I have come to discover that this passage is most concerned, not about a present securing a future, but a future that arrives in the present. More is going on here than one might think. It all depends on how the reader translates the phrase "eternal life." In the Greek, the words are *zoe* (life) *aiownios* (eternal). Thus, many correctly, but inadequately, translate the phrase to mean a quantity of life . . . then (in the future). This reduces Christianity to a future-oriented religion, leaving little imagination about the significance of the present moment. But what if there is another way to translate *zoe aiownios*? A way that is equally faithful, while also opening some things up for us.

If you dig deeply enough, you'll discover a faithful interpretation of the Greek also reads:

For God so loved the world that he gave his one and only Son, that whoever believes in him shall not perish but have the life of the age to come.

In this rendering, the passage becomes more dynamic, disrupting our familiarity and opening us to new possibilities. I'm always up for that as long as I am true to the text and not reading into it my own preferences. To translate the phrase this way, then, means John 3:16 is not merely about a *quantity* of life . . . then, but a *quality* of life . . . *now.* The Gospel writer is helping us to see that eternal life is not solely a future acquisition. It begins now. Simultaneously, to perish is not solely a future reality, but also happens now. One can feel rather alive, yet be living a kind of death that culminates in a future bodily death.

Consider the following from both interpretations of *zoe aiownios*:

Eternal life: The present moving toward a future.

The life of the age to come: The future moving toward our present.

Another way to say it, making room for both translations:

Eternal life contains the "not yet" dimension of the Kingdom—there is a full consummation of the Kingdom of Heaven and earth that we still await. The *life of the age to come* contains the "already" dimension—there are moments in the present where God's future Kingdom arrives as first fruits in our midst (James 1:18). John 3 is an invitation to hold both of these at the same time. If our backward direction roots us in depth, our forward direction propels us in power.

Anticipation matters. Most Christians feel bored in faith. Boredom is often a reflection of a local church worship culture. Sundays can serve as a litmus test for spiritual hunger levels. A friend of mine once challenged me to imagine the Holy Spirit descending on Sunday morning, dipping a toe into the service (I know, the personification is a bit much here), and evaluating whether the culture of the room was really desirous for the Presence of God. Although no one is perceptive enough to know for sure, I do think there is something to be said about a plausible connection between healing/breakthrough/ministry and the anticipation level of the community for God to show up and move. Postmodern philosopher, Peter Rollins, wrote of creating environments *for God to give God*. I find most churches are devised in such a way where it's mostly just the preacher giving her/his thoughts.

In his first letter to the confused, but eager church in Corinth, Paul wrote, "The Kingdom of God does not depend on talk but on power." In other words, ideas really matter, but so does breakthrough. Our ideas merely open us up for the real thing to penetrate our lives—God. God uses stories, Scripture, narratives, testimony, parable, prophecy, and teaching in order to open human hearts to anticipate more of God's arrival in the present. This is the life of the age to come. When Luke tells the Church in Acts to spread the hope of Jesus in the world, he doesn't admonish them to "go witnessing." Rather, he calls them to "be witnesses" (Acts 1:18). Better put, something dynamic, drastic, and disruptive has happened in your life because of the Living God. Therefore, tell the world what has happened to you. Somehow through that testimony, God opens hearts to receive the same Gospel, and to get caught up in the drama of God's salvation.

Let me alleviate any assumptions. Too often, when it comes to anticipating the miraculous, the wonders, and the life that includes yet transcends human reason, the Church deviates into hype and sensationalism. I know many people who grew weary of traditions where frenzy and chaos became the goal of the gathering. Where no one leaves until things get a little crazy. This is not healthy. This is not inviting a free God to give God; this is not a spirituality of surprise. This is spiritual entitlement where God has to show up in a particular way in order for us to feel spiritually successful. I suspect this is what Paul was getting at when writing to the same church in Corinth about the nature of spiritual gifts (1 Corinthians 12-14). May the Church always reject the seduction toward spectacle.

The Scriptures present the ministry of Jesus as entirely normative. He doesn't appear to get caught up in hype and spectacle. He often tells people, for various reasons, to not tell anyone about the miracle that had just occurred in them. He prayed simple prayers like: "Be healed," and "Take your mat and walk," and "Your sins are forgiven." And then it happened. Jesus, the Savior of the world, models ministry on earth. For the Church interested in following Jesus, we must permit him to be our model. The Church is never a community built on hype. The Church is always a community built on hope. And our hope is that God is here, God is free, and that in the name of Jesus anything is possible. The Church is always that weird, awkward, and strange community willing to suspend impossibility. The Kingdom does not depend on talk, but power. And that begins with anticipation. Anticipation simply means expecting more of tomorrow, today. The life of the age to come—today.

Consider the following illustration to visualize this reality:

Consider the previous chapter on the backward direction. The invitation was not simply to understand our ancestry as looking back in time at how God moved (1a.), but believing that the same God who acted will act again fresh in our time (1b.). We trust (Gr. *pistis*) that the God who moved then is the God who moves now. Historically this trust is called faith. Similarly, on the forward direction we do not simply look ahead to the future in hope (2a.) void of anticipation of that future glimpse in our present. Rather, we anticipate that future beginning to move into our present moment (2b.). This is why we continue to believe in healing, renewal, forgiveness, and restoration. When we press into these future realities, we by faith seek to pull the future into the present. This is not anti-rational. This is trans-rational. Christianity is a trans-rational people seeking to faithfully live the way of Jesus in real time, believing that the God who acted in the past, and will act in the future is acting now in the present. We, therefore, are a people of Presence. People who seek the Presence of God tend to be more open to the power of God.

A simple question:

Where is the power of God showing up in your life?

Maybe a better question:

Where isn't the power of God showing up in your life (and you need it to)?

Maybe it's a health crisis you are facing. Maybe it's a cynicism you just can't shake. Maybe it's a relationship where there's resentment that's led to bitterness, that bitterness traps you in unforgiveness, and that unforgiveness weighs heavily around your neck in the form of inward shame, and repressed anger . . . and no one knows about it . . . but you know about it, and it's time to let that go. Breathe. Maybe it's a marriage that's on its last leg, and you need breakthrough. Maybe it's a longing for an injustice to be finally righted. Maybe it's a financial breakthrough, or a vocational breakthrough, or a housing breakthrough. Maybe it has to do with your kids, and your influence with them has reached as far as it can go, and you need God to speak to your son or your daughter. Maybe it's an addiction, and you no longer have it, but whatever it is has you. Christians are people of anticipation. We anticipate the Presence of God who is renewing all things. And this Presence of God comes to us in the form of trans-rational power.

The Christian posture is one oriented toward new creation. That is why we lean into the forward direction. Our new creation orientation informs how we live, imagine, and long for the world to be. The future informs our present. Since all of creation is headed toward renewal, Christians bear witness to this future hope by seeking to actualize it now (Romans 8:22).

This makes the non-violent movement within a Darwinian world plausible.

This makes the exhausting pursuit of access to clean water for all of the world plausible.

This makes the onerous quest for racial reconciliation plausible.

This makes the expense of adoption plausible.

This makes our initiation toward relational forgiveness plausible.

This makes the crazy beatitudes of Jesus plausible.

These defiant Kingdom acts within a culture of vanity offer a preview to the world of where history is headed. The Church is called to be those weird and peculiar people who rehearse the future, seeking to pull it into the present through faith in the Living, ever Present God. This anticipation begins in worship. Teacher, Jean-Jacque von Allmen, claimed, "every time the Church assembles . . . to proclaim the death of Christ (1 Corinthians 11:26), it proclaims also the end of the world and the failure of the world... Christian worship is the strongest denial that can be hurled in the face of the world's claim to provide (humans) with an effective and sufficient justification of their life."[55]

EXPANSIVE IDEA

> In essence, worship is a prophetic protest of the world's
> counterfeit programs for happiness. It re-members us with
> who is truly reigning, and where all of the world is headed.
> As it turns out, worship in both song and body is a big deal
> in rehearsing the future.

Anointing matters. Most Christians feel ordinary in life. You've never met an ordinary human. C.S. Lewis said something like this in his book, *The Weight of Glory*. The God who spoke creation into existence is the same God who indwells our being in Jesus' name. This means the power that animates the universe lives within us, and seeks to work through us. I think much of the stagnation in the contemporary church is not an issue of *access* to power, but proper *alignment* with it. Children of God are not in danger of losing God's love. We are in danger of losing God's anointing. This is why confession and repentance matter. They seek not to shame us, but to realign us back with reality—namely, the Triune God. Most Christians feel bored and ordinary due to misalignment with the values and flow of the Kingdom of God. Jesus teaches this often when his disciples can't sort out why they, at times, did not heal.

Church history scholar, Alan Kreider, argues that the early Church believed anyone could heal.[56] He cites the early Church theologian, Irenaeus: "These prayers were frequently efficacious."[57] Further, Kreider claims that healing—the life of the age to come—was not an aberration in the Church; it was normative.[58] To be fair, he reminds his readers that Christians also suffered pain and loss to the same degree (sometimes more) than the pagan Roman world. Our belief that future renewal can, in part, be pulled into the present does not entitle us to that future, nor make it formulaic. Like the water of the pool at Siloam, sometimes the angels stir, and sometimes they don't (John 9). Our role is to align ourselves with the character of the Kingdom and anticipate God showing up in whatever way God desires. Make no mistake; the Holy Spirit anoints those who are willing to commit their lives to the way of Jesus. It seems that everywhere these people go, they bring with them the gifts of joy, hope, and love, even when they are unaware.[59]

Authority matters. Most Christians fear power at large. And who could blame them? Power structures throughout human history have exploited positions and resources for personal gain. Governments, institutions, corporations, and, yes, churches have abused power and caused suppression of the human spirit. This exploitation of power causes many to distrust authority completely, viewing it as entirely negative. The Church must regain a healthy definition and implementation of spiritual authority. Before his ascension, essentially his famous last words, Jesus reveals that all authority has been given to him. He then turns to his followers and empowers them to act on earth in his name (Matthew 28:18). What is happening here is that Jesus is entrusting the authority given to him to his people. The Kingdom of God is entrusted to those who will steward it for God's glory and other's good. The Church (personally and collectively) will give an account for the stewardship of this mystery. Every follower of Jesus has a measure of authority, which God has invested into her. Spiritual gifts and offices are the fruit of this authority. How we utilize these gifts, our influence, our resources, and positions matter significantly to the heart of God who has given us every good thing.

For members of the local church to walk in authority, patterned after the forward direction, means we should expect incredible things from the local church through the power of God. Christians have authority, and one of the roles of the pastoral staff is to empower the church to be the church in every given context.

Authentic spiritual power is always the result of being under authority. Missiologists Lois Barret and Darrell Guder wrote in their seminal work, *Missional Church*:

One exercises authority only insofar as one is under authority. The source of Jesus' authority lay not in the powers he had as divine. His authority sprang from his own faithful trust and loyalty, his living under authority . . . Jesus' healings, exorcisms, calming of storms, feeding of the multitudes, and raising the dead to life were all signs. These signs revealed that in Jesus' life under the authority of God the reign of God was at hand.[60]

Many Christians can nod their heads in theoretical agreement with Guder's words, yet feel light years away practically. Could it be that the most tragic consequence in the late modern quest for individualism[61] is being severed from the power and authority we were made to operate from? The quest for individualism always limits our capacity for true spiritual power because it untethers us from external resources. In this worldview, we fend for ourselves. This is why intimacy with God every day is the most empowered place to be in the world. This is why worship matters. This is why community matters.

Authentic spiritual power is when we channel the authority of God in us toward the good of another. True power is not self-directed, or self-centric, or self-seeking. Jesus always directed his power toward the good of the other rather than exploiting it for his own purpose. We access the power of the Spirit only so far as we come under the authority of the Risen Christ. We don't achieve it; we receive it, and then we are commissioned to release it for the advancement of the Kingdom of God in society. Jesus' teachings reveal that his followers have varying levels of authority. The question isn't: "What level of authority do you have;" the question is: "Where in life are you using the authority God has already given you?

Years ago I took a position in a major city as the Lead Pastor of a growing church whose founder was incredibly gifted at teaching and leadership. It was a tall task. As you might expect, proving myself was like always having a monologue in my head. It was crushing. One evening a young leader approached me with what she called "a word of knowledge." New to the charismatic, forward-oriented church world, I thought, "Lay it on me, sister. I'm ready." Expecting her to tell me that God had big plans for me, that I would be significant, and that this church will continue to grow, she handed me a slip of paper. It said one word: Cauliflower.

What a disappointment! Cauliflower?! When I think of this often neglected vegetable the following descriptives come to mind: bland, garnish, forgettable. Yet, there was something about that word that seemed particularly resonant in my soul. So I hung onto it. I placed the card in my briefcase. Every time I reached in for my computer, there it was, reminding me, haunting me, taunting me. What could it mean? Was God really in this?

Months later the word of knowledge found its meaning in my life. Teaching on the spiritual gifts, it dawned on me. Cauliflower means: AJ, you are not *the* gift. You are called to raise up the gifts. I love my Church!

It was good news. It saved me from attempting spectacle in my teaching week after week. It saved me from trying to replace someone and fill their shoes. It saved me from making the church about me. It saved a lot of people, I think. God was asking me to use my authority in such a way that ensured others could use theirs. What a call. The Church has authority. It must not be stifled. The gifts, and voices, and talents, and resources must be poured out so that the world may once again become full of the knowledge and love of God.

"The end is where we start from." T.S. Eliot once wrote that; I think he was right. We must ask where history is headed and then shape our life pursuits accordingly. We look forward to the full consummation of the Kingdom of Heaven on earth. But we then seek to glimpse that fullness in the present moment. We do this through faith that the God who has moved and will move is moving among us, dipping a toe in the local church, whispering, "They who really seek my Presence will never return disappointed."

EXPANSIVE PRACTICE ───────────────────────

The next time a person tells you about a struggle they are having, a conflict they are in, or a crisis they are facing, dare to lay a hand of them and pray a short but specific prayer over them in Jesus' name—right then and there. Practice acting as an agent of the Kingdom of God, who has been given anointing and authority. Decide to live without fear of (hu)man. Then see what happens.

EIGHT

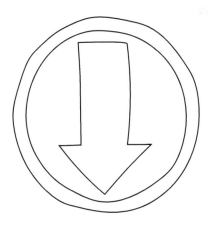

Downward

You are wanting to climb a great mountain and the good
God is trying to make you descend it; he is waiting for you
at the bottom in the fertile valley of humility.

Therese of Lisieux

"Don't touch it!" she exclaimed with a not-so-insignificant amount of disdain. She was an attractive woman. Yet, when she said it, her face deformed into the shape of utter disgust. It wasn't pretty. Frowning never is.

It was like Smeagol morphing into Gollum. Not that Smeagol was ever a sight for sore eyes, but you get the point. And it was my fault. I had failed her in that moment. The disdain, disgust, and anger were all aimed at me.

The year 2008 greeted the West to an unwelcome, but in some ways deserved, recession. I had come to the end of a paid sabbatical and had no ministerial assignments in sight. I was days from unemployment. So, I hit the pavement in hopes of serving tables. There was this ritzy wine bar down the street I thought would be fun to work at . . . for a short time anyway. I waltzed in and applied. After a brief conversation with the manager he placed a laptop on the bar and asked if I'd be willing to take a corporate compatibility test. I failed the compatibility test. Who knows why? But he gave me the job anyway. It wasn't that I was proficient at wine. I think they were just desperate for workers.

The establishment was located in a wealthier area of Atlanta, Georgia. It attracted a brand of clientele accustomed to "lunching." They were known as "Buckhead Bettys"—a cadre of local women who made fine dining look as natural as breathing. Each weekday they packed out the bar area in search of low calorie appetizers paired with bottomless bottles of Pinot Noir. And it my job was to serve them . . . and get paid.

She asked for a bottle of our finest Pinot Noir, and insisted it be placed on ice for 20 minutes before serving. Red wine, served slightly under room temperature, is the optimal condition for wine connoisseurs. In fact, European wine cellars are often located under the house to ensure red wine is served just under room temperature. She obviously knew what she was doing. So I fetched the Pinot and a bucket of ice.

I wasn't raised a wine guy, but I was a quick study. Far from the status of a sommelier, my expertise had been more theological than viticultural. Yet weeks into the job, to my surprise, guests were requesting to sit in my section. It felt pretty good, I'll be honest.

Two glasses in, the woman requested water. We had these black straws wrapped in cellophane packaging. Rather than extracting the straw myself, my habit was to pull back the cellophane and invite the guest to pull the straw for themselves. No one wants to ingest their server's germs. I get it. You probably do too.

And then it happened. Like muscle memory, without even looking at me . . . without acknowledging my humanity . . . without noticing the fine attention to detail I executed to ensure there was no germ transfer she exclaimed, "Don't touch it!" The very thing I was committed to getting correct, not touching the straw, was what she was afraid of. And her fear drove her to a reaction that left her face contorted and my feelings humiliated. All of this in public.

I went back to the kitchen and thought maybe I was just being over-sensitive. And then I thought, no, she simply dehumanized me. That really sucks. I felt humiliated. In the grand scheme of historic humiliation—the Israelites under Pharaoh, Jesus hanging naked on a thieves cross, the early Christians in Rome, the Jews in Nazi Germany, the gulags of Siberia, and the Jim Crow laws in America—this was small potatoes. Yet, the sting of humiliation was still real.

The culture in most restaurant kitchens isn't edifying. Often servers will put on a kind face in front of guests while cursing them in the kitchen. This wine bar was no asterisk. My temptation was to return to the kitchen and dehumanize her behind her back. Just before reaching the threshold of where the dining area meets the kitchen I saw a co-worker who would gladly receive my pain and join my commiseration. But just before the words came out of my mouth, I sensed the Holy Spirit whisper into my heart, "I'm the one who humanizes you. You don't need the world's approval." Further, I sensed that God loved this woman beyond what I could ever imagine. So I kept my mouth shut, and asked for joy to serve her well.

It was one of my finer moments. I wish I could say that my reactions were always so pure in heart. But that wouldn't be true. This is why the contents of this book matter. We are called to stretch into Christ's likeness over the course of a lifetime. This is the central human vocation.

I was humiliated. But when you know that you are loved by God, humiliation can become a pathway to greater Christlikeness. That does not mean we enjoy it, seek it, or make peace with the way injustice in the world can humiliate the powerless. It does mean that God is in the midst of every situation, and our response is tethered to humility that seeks to carry the cross that God may be exalted. It does mean that no matter who dehumanizes us, Christians are called to protest through love and not revenge. No one has modeled this out more for the modern world than Dr. Martin Luther King, Jr. As he followed the way of Jesus, he stood for his convictions, but stood in them humbly, turning the other cheek, carrying his cross, and non-violently leading people in a movement of human dignity for all.

My friend, Scott Sauls, is a pastor. In his book, *Befriend*, he writes, "The best way to measure your desire to serve is to look at how you respond when someone treats you like their servant." The litmus test for humility is revealed in every day situations. If you want to know whether you are growing into a humble person, listen to your life. Your life is a great teacher.

The pattern of Jesus' life can be viewed as one long descent over the course of thirty some-odd years. Marked by humility, his descent crescendoed at Golgotha. Several days before that historic pivot point in human history, Jesus performed a peculiar action that may still astound any reader willing to listen to the thirteenth chapter in the Gospel of John.

It was just before the Passover Festival. Jesus knew that the hour had come for him to leave this world and go to the Father. Having loved his own who were in the world, he loved them to the end. The evening meal was in progress, and the devil had already prompted Judas, the son of Simon Iscariot, to betray Jesus. Jesus knew that the Father had put all things under his power, and that he had come from God and was returning to God; so he got up from the meal, took off his outer clothing, and wrapped a towel around his waist. After that, he poured water into a basin and began to wash his disciples' feet, drying them with the towel that was wrapped around him (John 13:1-5).

Jesus is nearing the end. He knows it. He can feel the conspiracy closing in on him, and his adversaries are thirsty for blood . . . his blood. I would have run. Instead, he takes out a cloth and gets on his knees. The humility of it all. This is what real power does.

Real power doesn't exploit.

Real power doesn't dehumanize.

Real power doesn't shame.

Real power wraps a towel around its waist and washes feet.

That's nuts. Jesus . . . was . . . nuts!

Following Jesus shouldn't make you normal in the world. Following Jesus should make you nuts. Or as Paul put it: "We are the refuse of the world" (1 Corinthians 4). Many church traditions are so challenged by this specific moment in Jesus' life that they intentionally recall this story every year. It's known as *Maundy Thursday*. Radical acts of humility like these confront our tendencies to drift toward self-interest, comfort, and the insular life. The great writer, Ronald Rolheiser, describes this moment as, "The master taking the mantle of privilege and reversing it into the apron of service."[63] To live for someone else's well-being is the way of Jesus. Time and again the Scriptures confront us with this reality. Amidst a world that frequently inverts the meaning of life, Jesus reveals the path to flourishing is always others-oriented.

SCAFFOLDING

When in Bethlehem, be sure to walk through "the door of humility." Upon entering the Church of the Nativity, the location many claim Jesus was born, there is an entrance best suited for children . . . and hobbits. It measures around four feet high and two feet wide. To enter the holy site the average adult must first bow down. The inconvenience of the door reveals a core spiritual truth: bowing down in humility is the gateway to any real spirituality.

Likewise, how humbling it must have been for wise men from the East to fall prostrate toward the Christ child all of those years ago. How humbling it must have been for Mary and Joseph to receive false accusations about the nature of her pregnancy. After the resurrection, Jesus asks Peter three times in front of his friends if he loves him. That's embarrassing. Paul is struck blind for 3 days before he begins to truly see. Our egos are often so developed that it takes a crisis to get our attention. Humility somehow opens avenues for God to do deep work in us. Vision may inspire, and determination gets stuff done, but humility builds character. It seems that our spiritual heroes all traversed the path of humility at some point in life.

To cap it off, how humbling it must have been for God's first experience in flesh to be born in a cave for animals and placed in a feeding trough as a crib.

Consider our first act of worship to God. Christians are marked by baptism. What is baptism? It's an act of humble dependence before a God who must raise us up.

EXPANSIVE IDEA

When you think about it, it is strange that we are not called to do something great in our first response to God's lavish grace. Rather, we are called to receive the baptism of humility.

We go down into the waters, symbolically dying to ourselves, and are raised into newness in life. No one baptizes himself. We need someone else to take us down and then lift us up out of the water. This symbol reveals our need for God to lift us up to new heights we cannot achieve on our own. Baptism, then, is the initial plunge into a life of increasing humility. As we age, our humility should ever be increasing if we are following Jesus.

Before Dietrich Bonhoeffer, the 20th century German theologian, was captured by Nazi Germany for resistance to Adolf Hitler and his regime, he presciently wrote, "When Christ call a man, he bids him come and die."[64] This is the meaning of baptism. When we are baptized our bodies humbly enact God's exaltation, our self-limitation, and an outward orientation. We die on every level that we might rise again at even greater levels than previously imagined.

Ironically, humility is the posture that most fully reclaims the divinity that God has placed inside of us. We were made to dwell with God forever. This means God's original intent for us was both human and divine. To be human was intended to be divine. This doesn't mean you are God. The claim of the resurrection at the end of days means that our humanity will rise up and be cloaked with divinity . . . and we will reign with God forever and ever. This is huge. Jesus showed us that the pathway to divinity is always through the door of humility. In his letter to the local church in Philippi, Paul demonstrates that Jesus is both our model and invitation into this way of life. Consider this incredible invitation from Philippians 2:5-11:

> *In your relationships with one another, have the same mindset as Christ Jesus:*
>
> *Who, being in very nature God,*
> *did not consider equality with God*
> *something to be used to his own advantage;*
> *rather, he made himself nothing*
> *by taking the very nature of a servant,*
> *being made in human likeness.*
> *And being found in appearance as a man,*
> *he humbled himself by becoming obedient to death—*
> *even death on a cross!*
> *Therefore God exalted him to the highest place*
> *and gave him the name that is above every name,*
> *that at the name of Jesus every knee should bow,*
> *in heaven and on earth and under the earth,*
> *and every tongue acknowledge that Jesus Christ is Lord,*
> *to the glory of God the Father.*

Notice in verse 5 that Paul's vision is not merely vicarious. Jesus didn't embrace the way of humility to get us "off the hook" so to speak. Rather, it was a pattern we are called to step into. The cross of Christ was a unique apex in human history where the Son of God bore the sins of the world, which no one else could accomplish. Yet, our invitation is to be like him in humbly receiving all of the little deaths to our egos, our agendas, and our assumptions that can get in the way of dignifying others around us.

Remember, your identity is no longer in negotiation! You have been bought with the blood of Jesus. God's humility restored your dignity. Therefore, because you are a son/daughter of the Creator God, you no longer depend on others to honor you as a prerequisite to love them in return. This is liberating. Cooperating with the path of humility is our journey toward union with God. It best explains why Jesus said, *"Blessed are you when people insult you, persecute you and falsely say all kinds of evil against you because of me. Rejoice and be glad, because great is your reward in heaven, for in the same way they persecuted the prophets who were before you" (Matthew 5:11-12).* Because Jesus was humble, Christianity is a faith of humility. In our humility we dignify the world, even when we are being dehumanized.

Many believe the second chapter of Philippians was captured from a hymn of early Christians. This song grounded them in the story of Jesus—a story of descent that leads to ascent. A story that paradoxically proclaims the way down is the way up. It has been said that Scripture (correctly translated) never says Jesus "rose" from the dead. Rather, that Jesus "was raised" from the dead. The significance of this cannot be overstated. Jesus emptied himself to the nakedness of utter dependence on the Father. This is why he felt forsaken on the cross. He had nothing to cling to but trust/faith that the Father would resurrect him. Jesus' humility reached the abysmal depths of powerlessness. It is only in that place that resurrection truly takes place. Resurrection occurs from the place of self-offering and human weakness. It is there that only God (and not ourselves) has the power to act. Jesus modeled for us a willingness (active) to go down in order to powerfully come up (passive).

You must choose to go downward. The promise of "being raised" extends to all who willingly trust a resurrecting God. This is the paradoxical nature of Christian dynamism. No other religion, philosophy, or worldview has even been able to rival its profundity. The problem isn't the claims of Christianity, but Christians who are unwilling to embody the way of humility. For those Christians who have attempted to live this way out, we are utterly grateful for the effects they have had on liberation from racism, bigotry, sexism, fascism, and every form of unjust power that seeks to dominate God's original purposes. But you have to willfully choose downward and God will, in due time, lift you up.

Regarding the four cardinal virtues, a novice once asked Bernard of Clairvaux, the 12-century Cistercian monk, what he believed were their correct ordering in priority. Answering, he said, "Humility, humility, humility and humility. You alone can do it, but you cannot do it alone."[65] The monastic wisdom has always provided this insight. Humility is central to life in Jesus. Somewhere along the path of modernity, Christians have forgotten this. Humility has become an option rather than a mandate and *a pathway* rather than *the path*.

The monks of Christian history taught us that the way to know we were progressing in our faith was to ascend higher on the ladder of humility from one year to the next.[66] That means that embracing an orientation of "willingness" in life marks a mature believer more than "willfulness." Being willing to lose is one of the surest marks of a maturing follower of Jesus. Remember when Jesus, according to John's Gospel, told Peter that as he aged (presumably meaning as he matured in faith) he would no longer dress himself and go where he wanted. Rather, he would be told where to go (John 21:18)? This is a message for us all. As we age in the faith, our posture toward "willing humility" should grow. Saint Therese of Lisieux once counseled a novice, "You are wanting to climb a great mountain and the good God is trying to make you descend it; he is waiting for you at the bottom in the fertile valley of humility."[67]

The Original Flying V

Watching *The Mighty Ducks* was ritualized as an annual tradition at the Sherrill family reunions. Most of my cousins were raised fundamentalist Christians, which meant watching *Smurfs* was out of the question due to its ostensible Satanic implications. Yet for some reason *The Mighty Ducks* were deemed just holy enough for the whole family to absorb its plot into our souls annually. If you've seen the fictitious hockey film, then you know the secret weapon of the unlikely heroes—a V-shaped formation assisting the team in advancing the puck forward to score the winning goal. It was unexpected. But in the end it got the job done. According to Paul, Jesus lived a kind of V-shaped pattern of his own. Consider the following paradigm presented from the second chapter of Philippians.

Philippians 2

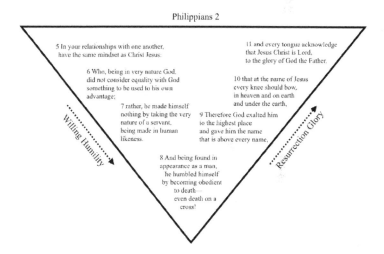

Indulge me as I nerd out a bit for the next 2 paragraphs. In an ironic twist, Paul presents Jesus as living a pattern of humility as the true path to glory. Within the political power structure of Rome, and the religious power structure of Israel, this was a subversive move. To fly, spiritually speaking, is to live in resurrected glory. The Eastern tradition calls this *theosis*. *Theosis* means we were meant to be like God, partaking in God's divine nature (2 Peter 1:4). This does not mean we ever replace God, but that we reflect God in both image and likeness. But the question is: How do we get there? The Philippian hymn unveils that the pathway to *theosis* (divinization) is paradoxically through what is known as *kenosis*.

Succinctly put: *Theosis* is the goal. *Kenosis* is the path. Let me explain.

Paul writes in Philippians 2:7 that Christ has "made himself nothing." The root word for this in Greek is *ken-a-o*. It can also be translated "emptied." From that term we get *kenosis*. The idea is that Jesus' life ended in exaltation, glory, and resurrection—namely, *theosis*.

EXPANSIVE IDEA

But the path to *theosis* was paradoxically not through self-exaltation or the modern views of success. Rather, it resulted from self-emptying, self-denial—namely, humility. This is the mystery of the ages. The way down is the way up. *Kenosis* leads to *theosis*. Humility is the only sure path to glory.

Humans rarely believe this. Which is why pride is the cardinal sin that sets into motion all other sins.

Martin Luther, the 16th century German professor, once wrote:

Faith makes us lords, love makes us servants; aye, through faith we become gods and partakers of the divine nature and name, as Ps. 82:6 says: I have said, 'Ye are gods; and all of you are children of the Most High.' But through love we become equals of the very lowliest. According to faith we are in need of nothing but have a sufficiency of everything; according to love we serve everybody. Through faith we receive gifts from above, from God; through love we dispense them downward to our neighbor. Just so Christ was in need of nothing according to His divinity, but according to His humanity He served everybody who was in need of Him.[68]

Perhaps like you, I am interested in resurrection life . . . now. I believe that Jesus' resurrection is the first fruit pointing to the future of creation. But I also believe that there are moments in the present where signs of resurrection burst forth. The question then arises: How does one begin to experience this resurrection kind of life in the present? The answer to that most simply (and paradoxically) is through the downward direction. Resurrection life happens out of our weakness and self-offering—it is there that only God (and not ourselves) has the power to act.

EXPANSIVE PRACTICE ─────────────────────

In 2016 some friends of mine were invited to the Vatican to discuss Church unity with Pope Francis. Even more astonishing than that, my friends are Protestants. For two hours they discussed essential matters concerning the future of the Church. They said it was unlike any conversation they had ever been invited to. One of them asked the Holy Father what ministry is most important in the world in which we live. Pope Francis gave it some thought, and with conviction asserted, "The ministry of the ear." In a world of incessant sound bites and constant opinions, what the world needs most of all is a communion who will listen, learn, and love. When I heard this I thought of Bernard's seminal virtue—humility.

In every small group I am a part of, I imagine this cloud hovering over my head. Within the cloud a number is displayed. With every word I use that number climbs. This is all make-believe of course. I like to think that I permit those in the group to display higher word counts than me. The problem is that I'm a talker and I enjoy expressing my opinion . . . and I have many opinions of any given subject matter. But there comes a time when it is better for me to listen, to seek solidarity, to find common ground, and to understand rather than being understood. Can you think of one person to whom you should listen more carefully? Can you think of a place or a group that you are a part of where you need to speak less? This is one simple act of humility you can do this week.

Jesus listened often. He would also provoke others to speak, saying things like: "What do you want me to do for you?" That's humility. That's solidarity. That's the beginning of downward. That's the beginning of love. To expand into Christlikeness demands we follow him down to the least of these in the world.

ENDNOTES

1. Richard J. Foster and Grover Gardner, Celebration of Discipline: The Path to Spiritual Growth (Blackstone Audio Inc., 2013), 1.

2. Bill Hull, Jesus Christ, Disciplemaker (Grand Rapids, MI: Baker Books, 2004).

3. Dustin Allen, "Out of the Bungalow: An Interview with Bon Iver. http://www.treblezine.com/out-of-the-bungalow-bon-iver-interview/ (accessed October 23, 2017).

4. Cal Newport, Deep Work: Rules for Focused Success in a Distracted World (New York: Grand Central Publishing, 2016), Kindle Edition, 4.

5. David Brooks, The Road to Character (New York: Random House Publishing Group, 2015), Kindle Edition, locations 101-107.

6. Søren Kierkegaard, Howard Vincent Hong, Edna Hatlestad Hong, and George Pattison, Works of Love (New York: Harper-Perennial, 2009), 22.

7. Henri Nouwen, "Moving from Solitude to Community to Ministry," www.leadershipjournal.net (1995): 81.

8. Mark Thibodeaux, S.J., Armchair Mystic: Easing into Contemplative Prayer (Cincinnati, OH: St. Anthony Messenger Press, 2011), Kindle Edition, 41-42.

9. Quoted in Sherry Turkle and Kirsten Potter, Reclaiming Conversation: The Power of Talk in a Digital Age (New York, Penguin Press, 2015), 78.

10. Ibid.

11. Dietrich Bonhoeffer, Letters and Papers from Prison (New York: Macmillan Publishing Co., 1971), 418–419.

12. Martin Laird, A Sunlit Absence: Silence, Awareness, and Contemplation (New York: Oxford University Press, 2011), Kindle Edition, 42.

13. Brandon Griggs, "Jon Stewart, In His Own Words," http://www.cnn.com/2015/08/05/entertainment/jon-stewart-wit-wisdom-feat/index.html (accessed October 23, 2017).

14. Nouwen, "Moving from Solitude to Community to Ministry," 81.

15. Turkle and Potter, Reclaiming Conversation, 42.

16. Ibid.

17. Malcolm Muggeridge, Conversion: A Spiritual Journey (London: Hodder & Stoughton, 1996), 22.

18. Brennan Manning, The Signature of Jesus (Colorado Springs, CO: Multnomah Books, 2013), 212.

19. Julian Treasure, "Five Ways to Listen Better," https://www.ted.com/talks/julian_treasure_5_ways _to_listen_better (accessed October 23, 2017).

20. Henri J.M. Nouwen, Life of the Beloved: Spiritual Living in a Secular World (New York: Crossroad Pub. Co, 2002), 133.

21. Quoted in Laird, A Sunlit Absence, 60.

22. A sabbatical is like an extended vacation for pastors every 7 years where we read books beyond our comprehension, drink even more coffee than usual, and attempt to write books we have no intention to finish—and that few would ever want to read.

23. Later I discovered that sometimes even God's "absence" is a kind of presence, driving us into deeper pursuit.

24. Thanks Chris.

25. In Latin, this is known as Homo Incurvatus.

26. Aglow International, "Seven Hebrew Words for Praise," https://www.aglow.org/images/leaderDev/seven-praise-words.pdf.

27. David W. Fagerberg, On Liturgical Asceticism (Washington, DC: The Catholic University of America Press, 2013), 23.

28. Ibid.

29. Simon Chan, Liturgical Theology: The Church as Worshiping Community (Downers Grove, IL: InterVarsity Press, 2006, 43.

30. James K.A. Smith, Imagining the Kingdom: How Worship Works (Grand Rapids, MI: Baker Academic, 2013).

31. Jean-Jacques von Allmen, Worship: Its Theology and Practice (London: Lutterworth, 1966), 63.

32. Representing the whole body of Christ, and not just a part.

33. Martin Luther and Mark D. Tranvik, The Freedom of a Christian (Minneapolis: Fortress Press, 2008).

34. Walter Wink, "History Belongs to the Intercessors," https://celectcdn.s3.amazonaws.com/files/0024/ 6892/2012.01.08.pastors_blog.pdf (accessed October 23, 2017).

35. Quora.com, https://www.quora.com/Do-fungi-carry-out-photosynthesis (accessed October 23, 2017).

36. For a scholarly analysis on how culturally humiliating and physically excruciating, see The Crucifixion by Fleming Rutledge.

37. For example, Vibia Perpetua who was excommunicated from her family and martyred in 203AD.

38. Kate Murphy, "Do Your Friends Actually Like You?" The New York Times (August 6, 2016), https://www.nytimes.com/2016/08/07/opinion/sunday/do-your-friends-actually-like-you.html (accessed October 23, 2017).

39. Benedicta Ward, trans., The Sayings of the Desert Fathers: The Alphabetical Collection (Kalamazoo, MI: Cistercian, 2004).

40. Larry W. Hurtado, Destroyer of the Gods: Early Christian Distinctiveness in the Roman World (Waco, TX: Baylor University Press, 2017).

41. Chris Colin, "The Incredibly True Story of Renting a Friend in Tokyo," https://www.afar.com/magazine/the-incredibly-true-story-of-renting-a-friend-in-tokyo (accessed October 23, 2017).

42. Dalai Lama, Desmond Tutu, and Douglas Carlton Abrams, The Book of Joy: Lasting Happiness in a Changing World (New York: Penguin Publishing Group, 2016), Kindle Edition, 59-60

43. From podcast, Conversations with Tyler. Episode 25, "Ben Sasse on the Space between Nebraska and Neverland" (June 28, 2017).

44. Hurtado, Destroyer of the Gods, 176.

45. Sebastian Junger, Tribe: On Homecoming and Belonging (New York: Grand Central Publishing, 2016), Kindle Edition, 93.

46. Donald Miller said this at the Q Conference in Portland, Oregon, April 27, 2011.

47. Christena Cleveland, Disunity in Christ: Uncovering the Hidden Forces That Keep Us Apart (Colorado Springs, CO: Intervarsity Press, 2013).

48. Lama, Tutu, and Abrams, The Book of Joy, 130.

49. Ibid., 59-60.

50. Martin Luther King and Coretta Scott King, Strength to Love (Minneapolis: Fortress, 2010), 140.

51. Alexis de Tocqueville, "Democracy in America," http://xroads. virginia.edu/~hyper/DETOC/ch1_18.htm (accessed October 23, 2017).

52. Friedrich Nietzsche, "Beyond Good and Evil," https://www. marxists.org/reference/archive/nietzsche/ 1886/beyond-good-evil/ch05.htm (accessed October 23, 2017).

53. Rutledge, The Crucifixion, 217.

54. David Hayward, http://www.nakedpastor.com.

55. Von Allmen, Worship, 63.

56. Alan Kreider, The Patient Ferment of the Early Church: The Improbable Rise of Christianity in the Roman Empire (Grand Rapids, MI: Baker Academic, 2016), 112.

57. Irenaeus, Haer 2.32.4, trans. A. Roberts, ANF 1:409.

58. Kreider, The Patient Ferment of the Early Church, 112.

59. As was the case with Mother Teresa of Calcutta.

60. Lois Barrett and Darrell L. Guder, Missional Church: A Vision for the Sending of the Church in North America (Grand Rapids, MI: William B. Eerdmans, 2009).

61. Individualism is a worldview that rejects the reality of God as necessary for daily life. It places ultimate value on subjective experience. This is the greatest idol in the modern era.

62. Scott Sauls, Befriend (New York: Tyndale House Publishers, 2016), 8.

63. Ronald Rolheiser, Sacred Fire (New York: Random House, 2014), 121.

64. Dietrich Bonhoeffer, The Cost of Discipleship (New York: Macmillan, 1963).

65. Ernest Kurtz and Katherine Ketcham, The Spirituality of Imperfection: Storytelling and the Search for Meaning (New York; Bantam Press, 2009), 185.

66. Greg Peters, The Story of Monasticism: Retrieving an Ancient Tradition for Contemporary Spirituality (Grand Rapids, MI: Baker Publishing Group, 2009), Kindle Edition, 76.

67. Mary Victorious, "Humility the Great Virtue," http://maryvictorious.blogspot.com/2009/04/humility-great-virtue.html (accessed October 23, 2017).

68. Michael J. Christensen and Jeffery A. Wittung, Partakers of the Divine Nature: The History and Development of Deification in the Christian Traditions (Grand Rapids, MI: Baker Academic, 2008).

86234398R00067

Made in the USA
Columbia, SC
30 December 2017